Hans Frei and Edward Schillebeeckx

A Conversation on Method and Christology

Editions SR / Éditions SR

Editions SR / Éditions SR is a general series of books in the study of religion, encompassing the fields of study of the constituent societies of the Canadian Corporation for Studies in Religion / Corporation canadienne des sciences religieuses. These societies are: Canadian Society of Biblical Studies / Société canadienne des études bibliques; Canadian Society of Church History / Société canadienne de l'histoire de l'église; Canadian Society of Patristic Studies / Association canadienne des études patristiques; Canadian Society for the Study of Religion / Société canadienne pour l'étude de la religion; Canadian Theological Society; Société canadienne de théologie; and Société québécoise pour l'étude de la religion.

GENERAL EDITORS: *H. Martin Rumscheidt and Theodore S. de Bruyn*

Editions SR

Volume 26

Hans Frei and Edward Schillebeeckx

A Conversation on Method and Christology

Marguerite Thabit Abdul-Masih

Published for the Canadian Corporation for Studies in Religion /
Corporation Canadienne des Sciences Religieuses
by Wilfrid Laurier University Press

2001

This book has been published with the help of a grant from the Humanities and Social Sciences Federation of Canada, using funds provided by the Social Sciences and Humanities Research Council of Canada. We acknowledge the financial support of the Government of Canada through the Book Publishing Industry Development Program for our publishing activities.

National Library of Canada Cataloguing in Publication Data

Abdul-Masih, Marguerite Thabit, 1956-
    Edward Schillebeeckx and Hans Frei : a conversation on method and Christology

(Editions SR; v. 26)
Includes bibliographical references and index.
ISBN 0-88920-376-8

1. Theology—Methodology. 2. Experience (Religion). 3. Jesus Christ—History of doctrines. 4. Frei, Hans W. 5. Schillebeeckx, Edward, 1914- I. Canadian Corporation for Studies in Religion. II. Title. III. Series

BT202.A23 2001   230'.01   C2001-903139-4

Cover design by Leslie Macredie.

∞

Printed in Canada

Order from:

Wilfrid Laurier University Press
Waterloo, Ontario, Canada N2L 3C5

CONTENTS

INTRODUCTION

Any contemporary theological work must start with a description of its method. In working out such a description, however, we are concerned not only with answering how a particular theological task is done, but also with the theological reasoning justifying the method being adopted. For theological reasoning encompasses the fundamental presuppositions of the theologian.

The contemporary concern for method includes a change in the understanding of the task of theology. With the Enlightenment, theology no longer limited itself to the task of explaining "revealed truths," but had to address also the human concern for ultimate reality and meaning within historical contexts. In particular during the Enlightenment, two main shifts in human reasoning occurred that are related to each other. One shift was the dawn of the scientific revolution and as a result the ascendency of the scientific method. This shift was accompanied by a parallel change in philosophical reasoning which is usually called the "turn to the subject."

With the rise of the scientific revolution, the scientific method became prevalent. The scientific method was based on experimentation and inductive reasoning. Intellectual inquiry starts from particular observed phenomena through nature or through experimentation, and then proceeds to generalizations or laws. One no longer starts with accepted truths but rather with particulars which are tested by experiments. The scientific method was not limited to the hard sciences; philosophy also adopted the scientific method. Philosophy no longer argues deductively from general premises to particulars, but rather inductively from observed particulars to generalities.

Another major contribution of the Enlightenment was the "turn to the subject." Philosophy concerns itself with the question of meaning raised by the human subject. But now philosophical method starts with "experiments." However, a question arose: What do we mean by "experiments" in the realm of meaning? The answer was simple: turn to the subject since it is the subject who seeks meaning. Consequently another question arose: How can one speak of "experiments" of the "subject"? The answer was the introduction of the concept of "experience." In other words, what "experiments" is to "objects," "experience" is to "subjects." Or, put differently, "experience" is the scientific method applied to subjective questions such as meaning. The philosophical method now came into line with the scientific method. This is the genesis of the language of "experience."

Theological method in the wake of the Enlightenment, with its interest in scientific method and its interest in the subject, also adopted the category of "experience." It is important to note, however, that this turn to experience and the subject occurred mainly in Protestant circles, notably in the works of Schleiermacher, considered to be the father of modern theology. In Catholic theology it would take considerably longer to turn to "experience" and the "subject."

With the emphasis on the human subject and on "experience," theology no longer limited itself to explaining revealed truths about the divinity of Jesus Christ or the mystery of the Trinity, but also raised questions about the human relationship to God and God's relationship to humans. This relationship was seen as the point of religion. God was seen as one who speaks through the inmost human dimensions; that is, God was no longer seen as extrinsic to human reality but more intrinsic to it. God was not exclusively revealed in the Bible and in Jesus but also through human experience. In other words, changes in theological method affected the content of theological discourse.

These notions of "experience" and the "turn to the subject" had many implications for theology. One of the most important implications was a positive valuation of the human being. Human achievements — whether political, social economic or scientific — were seen in a very positive light. There was optimism in the air and a general trust in human capabilities. This optimism, however, had a major setback with the two great wars of the twentieth century. There arose a backlash against the liberal view of the human. The evil of human history was revealed. It was seen that theology had put the human on equal footing with God. Theologians such as Karl Barth called for a return to the supremacy of God, away from the "subject" and human "experience" as a basis for theology.

However, the debate has not abated. The function of experience in the construction of theology is still a central issue. Earlier on, this conflict was manifested in the controversy between Barth on the one hand and Bultmann, Tillich and others on the other. In more recent years this controversy has been seen in the debate between the Chicago School which advocates the "turn to the subject" in the form of "experience" and the Yale School which advocates a return to the original theological task of describing the faith of the Christian community.

The contemporary debate over "experience" in theological method concerns issues such as *what* constitutes the experience upon which theology must reflect, the subsequent question of *how* experience should be used, and finally *why* it should be used, that is, the reasons for the choice in the first place, whether those reasons are theological or philosophical.

Various theologians thus disagree on *what* constitutes the experience upon which theology must reflect. For a "cultural linguistic" theologian such as George Lindbeck, it is the external realities of the life of the church that should be the basis for all theological reflection and not private, individualistic or internal experience. For others, such as some liberation theologians, experience is understood as the political and economic experience of oppression and poverty and as the struggle to overcome it. Still others, such as some feminist theologians, though similar in outlook to the liberation theologians in their concentration on the experience of oppression, would concentrate more on the experience of oppression of women and how religious beliefs contributed to this oppression. For liberation and feminist theologians, experience is more of a secular type, that is, less connected with a certain religion or religious practice. Still others, such as the existentialist theologians Rahner and Macquarrie, understand experience more in terms of the personal internal dimensions of the human person. For such existentialist theologians, experience is described in subjective language and is understood and spoken of in transcendental terms. There is clearly no consensus on what is meant by experience.

However, even among those who have a similar outlook, such as feminist theologians, there is a spectrum of understandings of *how* experience should be used. There are diverse views on the relationship between experience on the one hand, and tradition and Scripture on the other, that is, of what constitutes the norms and sources of theology and what is understood by truth. Furthermore, issues such as the role of the historical-critical and literary-critical methods in biblical hermeneutics also are important to the question. Moreover, even when there is agreement on what is meant by experience, how it is used poses further questions.

We come now to the question of *why* experience is to be used. If we return to the question of what we mean by experience, we find that the answer depends not so much on experience per se, but rather on some theological position concerning issues such as revelation, grace and God's action. Thus, if revelation is understood as identical with Jesus Christ, and if one holds that only the church mediates Jesus Christ, then experience is seen as the life of the church that worships Jesus Christ. On the other hand, if revelation is understood in terms of God's activity mediated through human life and history in its entirety, then experience, whether existential or in terms of negative experience, becomes important to the revelatory moment.

The other aspect of the question "why use experience?" is related to the question of the purpose of the theological enterprise. Some propose that the purpose of the theological enterprise is to seek the relevance and connection between one's beliefs and the rest of one's life. Such theologians believe that, if our Christian beliefs are to be relevant, they must become relevant through constant dialogue with culture, and the only way to make Christian beliefs reasonable, accessible or relevant to contemporary individuals is to identify a connection between these beliefs and the experience of those persons who hold them. Moreover, the same theologians tend to hold that the Christian movement itself started with an experience, and that experience has been a source of theology all along. For such theologians, hermeneutics is of crucial importance, since hermeneutics is concerned with the question of how to interpret and understand Scripture and tradition in order that they become relevant and appropriate to our times. By contrast, there are theologians who claim that using experience as either a norm or a source for theology shifts the weight of theological authority from God to humanity, and from the Bible and Jesus Christ to the world, thus diluting the Christian message. For these theologians, Christianity then becomes merely another expression of the culture, rather than a radical critique of it. The two sides use not only theological arguments but also arguments from philosophy, psychology, sociology and literary criticism to expand and clarify their theological position.

The proposal put forth in this book consists of three points that are interrelated. The first point is that theological method is very much influenced by theological reasoning itself—that is, that what one believes about doctrines of revelation and God's activity will shape one's attitude towards experience. Convictions about revelation and divine activity will determine whether experience is necessary for theology proper, define in broad terms that which constitutes experience, and finally affect how experience is used.

The second point is that the attitude towards experience and its use will in turn shape the subsequent theology. In other words, what is proposed is a circular or spiral movement. Theological beliefs and propositions affect one's understanding of and attitude towards experience, i.e., what it is and how it is to be used, which further affects subsequent theological propositions, such as doctrines of Jesus Christ and the Trinity and so on.

The third point put forward is that the use of the category of "experience" is itself contextual. The purpose is not to adjudicate between different methods in theology that use or do not use the category of "experience." There is plurality in theological methods. Context influences the choice of the most appropriate method to address the questions raised but also to safeguard the proposed theological presuppositions.

To expand my proposal, I have chosen two authors, Hans Frei and Edward Schillebeeckx. The reason for my choice is that Frei and Schillebeeckx represent the tension in contemporary theology surrounding the issue of experience. Schillebeeckx holds that experience is the source for theological reflection, and furthermore that, with qualifications, it can act as a norm for theology. For Schillebeeckx, experience not only consists of what we usually mean by experience, that is, our daily encounter with others and the world, but also includes tradition and Scripture as other forms of experience. Schillebeeckx's theological reasons are based on his understanding of revelation and the place of God's activity in the world. He draws on several philosophical disciplines to help clarify his position, such as critical theory, existential philosophy, and analytical and language philosophy. Frei, on the other hand, does not agree with Schillebeeckx that experience should play a role in theology proper. Frei has his own theological reasons, which are again connected with the understanding of revelation. Frei believes that revelation is identical with Jesus Christ, and since theology is talk about God who is revealed in Jesus Christ, then theology itself is talk about Jesus Christ. In that sense Jesus is the norm and source for theology. As a result, experience has little value in talk about Jesus Christ. However, experience has a place in the "application" aspect of theology, such as in ethics and pastoral theology.

PART ONE

HANS FREI

1

DOCTRINAL CONSIDERATIONS:
THE DOCTRINE OF REVELATION

Before discussing Hans Frei's theological position, it may be helpful to mention something about his life and background (Hunsinger , private letter, 1992). Frei was born in Germany in 1922. Both his parents were physicians. His father taught at the University of Berlin and was a well-known immunologist. It is thought that he taught at the same university where Bonhoeffer's father also taught.

Although Frei's family was Jewish, they assumed an assimilated social status. The Kaiser bestowed this social status on the family, when Frei's great-uncle fought in the battle of Jena. Thus, the family became nominally Lutheran. Frei was baptized in the Prussian Union Church which was strongly influenced by the theology of Schleiermacher, and he had some religious affiliation as a youth.

In 1935, Frei was sent to the Friends' School, in Saffron Waldon in Essex, England, because of the political situation in Germany. He stayed there until 1938. It is thought that his sister went with him. In 1938, Frei, his mother and sister went to the United States. It is not clear whether his father and brother went with them or not. The family lived in dire poverty in an apartment in upper Manhattan. During this time his father died.

It seems that in 1938 Frei was sent on a scholarship to North Carolina State College to study textile engineering. There he appears to have been active in some sort of student Christian Fellowship. He received his B.Sc. from North Carolina. During

Frei's last year at North Carolina State College, H. Richard Niebuhr came and spoke at the college, on the basis of which Frei decided that he wanted to work with Niebuhr. He went to Yale Divinity School and received his B.D. in 1945.

For the following two years Frei served as minister in the First Baptist Church of North Stratford, New Hampshire. During this time he decided to become an Episcopalian. He taught briefly at Wabash College between 1950 and 1953 and then in the Episcopal Seminary of the Southwest from 1953 to 1957. In 1956 he completed his doctorate at Yale and joined its faculty, where he stayed until his death in 1988.

It is interesting to note that Frei was very much interested in Zionism yet was sympathetic to the Palestinian issue. Furthermore, he never discussed the Holocaust nor did he invest it with any revelatory significance. This was very much in line with his theology in which the experience of the Holocaust fit more with the *applicatio* rather than the *explicatio* or *meditatio* in the constructive work of Christian theology.

Let us turn now to Frei's understanding of revelation. Frei was not a systematic theologian but a specialist in the history of religious thought, so his concept of revelation is generally implicit in his works and rarely made explicit in a systematic way. In particular, Frei's understanding of revelation is inferred mainly from his early analysis of Barth's understanding of revelation and from his later writings about the necessity of the recovery of the literal sense of the Bible.

Although Frei takes much of his understanding of revelation from Barth, he introduces some nuances that reflect his conception of how the notion of revelation developed during the Enlightenment, as well as his proposed corrective to the situation of this development.

1.1 Revelation and the Enlightenment

According to Frei, the question of hermeneutics arose out of a shift in the understanding of revelation that occurred in the eighteenth century in England and Germany. This shift occurred in response to two questions. One question was concerned with the credibility of revelation in history and of miracles in particular; a second question was concerned with the likelihood of the occurrence of revelation. "Two issues were at stake from the beginning. The first was of a predominantly philosophical nature. It concerned the inherent rationality or credibility of the very idea of a historical revelation. Was it conceivable or intelligible? . . . The second question was: Even granted the rationality or inherent possibility of revelation, how likely is it that such a thing has actually taken place? This is no longer an issue of theoretical but of factual inquiry" (Frei 1974: 52-53). According to Frei's analysis, theologians in England and in Germany attempted to answer the questions of the credibility and factuality of revelation differently. Generally speaking, English thinkers proceeded to answer the questions using external and independent evidence, such as geology. Germans, on the other hand, proceeded with investigation of the internal evidence, i.e., literary-historical evidence (1974: 56). The two questions could be put differently: one was concerned with the *meaning* of revelation, which became the realm of hermeneutics; the other was concerned with the *occurrence* of revelation, which became the realm of historical investigation. A split thus resulted between hermeneutics and historical criticism. According to Frei, the result was that literal sense, historical fact and religious truth and meaning were set apart from each other.

For Frei, this development leads to a further question: Is revelation located in the fact *that* Jesus came, or is it concerned with *what* Jesus taught or meant? According to Frei, during the course of the eighteenth century, the locus of revelation shifted away from the fact *that* Jesus came to become *what* Jesus taught and meant. This split, Frei argues, between those who held that revelation was the fact *that* Jesus came and those who held that revelation resided in *what* Jesus taught and meant is the genesis of the problem of interpretation. In other words, the rise of hermeneutics was part of an attempt to locate revelation. He writes,

It is well to keep in mind that this literary-historical debate over the trustworthiness of history-like Biblical accounts both arose and abode over the claims about unique historical revelation, in particular that Jesus was the Messiah. One ought therefore to make a distinction between two connected "fact" issues, in theology as well as in Biblical exegesis. There is first the question, of the reliability of accounts involving physical miracles. . . . But secondly, the much more important issue: Is it really the meaning of the pertinent Biblical texts that the salvation of man depends not only on *what* Jesus taught and did, but on all this as an expression of the presumably indispensable fact, given by divine fiat and authority, *that* he existed, and existed as the Son of God incarnate? The latter is the exegetical and theological issue of "positivity" for Christian belief which has nagged theology ever since the latter part of the eighteenth century. (Frei 1974: 57)

Frei believes that the shift of the locus of revelation from the fact *that* Jesus Christ came to *what* Jesus Christ taught and meant was a direct result of the Enlightenment's questioning of all authority (especially religious authority) except that of reason. Thus, the question of the reliability and factuality of revelation was a result of the application of rational criteria to that which is religious.

The greatest influence here was that of Kant, and especially his assertions, first, that there is a distinction between a thing in itself and a thing in relation to us and, second, that practical reason is limited in its knowledge of God (Frei 1974: 284). This limitation of reason applies most importantly to our knowledge of God: God can be known only in relation to us. The effect of Kant on Christian theology can be seen on two related levels. First, Kant reinforces the idea that the locus of revelation is no longer the fact *that* Jesus came, for such language seeks to speak of God in God's self. Second, Kant encourages the shift to *what* Jesus taught and meant, for that teaching has a direct impact on us and is related to us. "It became a commonplace in nineteenth-century Protestant theology that we know God only under the qualification of a religious relation to him (be it revelation or some other), and not as he is in himself" (Frei 1974: 283-84).

For Frei, then, the outcome of the Enlightenment is that revelation is now interpreted as *relational*. Like Barth, Frei identifies Schleiermacher as the mediating theologian who correlated not only theology and philosophy, but also, on a deeper level, God and humanity. Frei also shares Barth's fear that this may lead to an understanding that sees God and the human as equals in this correlating process, with the result that theological statements lose their axiomatic character and can only be "proven" through the use of non-theological criteria.

> And then, toward the end, we listen to the same strain when [Barth] says that the Reformation correlation between Word of God or Jesus Christ, and faith becomes equated with the correlation between History and experience as the two foci of an ellipse for Schleiermacher. This is a favorite Barthian . . . metaphor for the reproach that divine grace or prevenience and human possibility are simply synergistically related in this theology, nullifying the central thrust of the Reformation, for which not only can "Word of God" and "faith" not be exchanged for any other terms but their "correlation" takes place only in the absolute priority of Word to faith. This is again a way of criticizing Schleiermacher's theology for its dual and interconnected Christological and epistemic deficiency. (Frei 1993: 181-82)

For Frei, Schleiermacher represents a type of theology in which one cannot speak of revelation except in relation to corporate religious consciousness. Thus, to understand revelation one must "turn to the subject" either through a focus on the consciousness or through a concentration on epistemology. Thus, the result of Kant's limitation of reason is that theologians "assumed that religion is a formal or a priori structure in terms of which certain particular experiences in history must be explained" (Frei 1975: 33). In other words, those theologians answer the question of revelation by seeking the condition of the possibility of receiving revelation in the human realm. The possibility of receiving revelation is an a priori structure of being human.

1.2 Frei's Appropriation of Barth

For an alternative model, Frei looks to Barth's proposal that revelation is God's free self-gift to humanity. As a free self-gift, it is the result of God's sovereign act. Revelation, therefore, is not and cannot be a *function* of humanity or human nature. "Revelation and Grace are God's sovereign acts, not constants of a relational datum" (Frei 1975: 40).

As we have already seen, Frei rejects "relational" revelation, because such a view fails to see that revelation is the self-communication of God, and reduces it to an aspect of anthropology. Instead of speaking of the sovereign freedom of God, the "relational" view of revelation makes God and the human into *equal* partners in this relationship, such that God may become the image of the human rather than a judge of humanity. Hence, Frei rejects relational revelation because it endangers the freedom of God, by seeing the focus of revelation as its human reception and acceptance. In this way, it allows God's revelation to be delimited by human understanding: God's self-communication becomes contingent on human freedom rather than on the freedom of God. Frei's fundamental concern is thus to conserve God's Lordship and freedom, which is restricted neither by God's self-communication nor by creation.

> Fundamental in [Barth's] concern is the acknowledgment of the freedom and Lordship of God. These qualities God affirms in his condescending grace. They are not restricted by creation or grace. It is the greatest perversion, therefore, to tie God "relationally" to any preconceived method, sup-

posedly the echo of a "symmetrical" relation between divine revelation and an independently gained concept of religion. Instead, one must insist that grace is sheer miracle which we can only "*ac*-knowledge." (Frei 1975: 41)

This means that Frei completely refocuses the question of the reception of revelation, arguing with Barth that in revelation God creates the possibility of revelation's own reception. The possibility of this reception is not an a priori condition or structure of the human; rather, revelation is like a meteorite which, falling from outer space and impacting against the ground, creates the crater that will receive it. In that sense God is the *subject* or agent of revelation and not its *object*. "The reality of the knowledge is based on God's self-revelation. The very question of its possibility [knowledge of God] can be raised only on the grounds of or posterior to its actuality" (1975: 51).

In his understanding of the reception of revelation, then, Frei takes up Barth's emphasis on the freedom of God. He writes: "Barth's overwhelmingly great conviction which persisted throughout the post-liberal days (over against Schleiermacher and the relationist, liberal tradition) was that of the sovereign freedom of God over his creation" (Frei 1956: 447). Of course, for Barth — and for Frei — God's freedom is freedom of love, to draw near and to be in relation to us. Thus, God is essentially one who is "towards" humans. But God's relation to us is an internal necessity rather than a necessity imposed on God externally: God is related to us not because of who we are but rather because of the nature of God's own being. By contrast, in relational revelation, God is related to us (whether as a condition of our possibility or as an existential of our being) in such a way that the human condition becomes an external necessity for revelation, and the freedom of God is compromised. As Frei puts it: "The relation of God to man is not a reversible relation. God is not present in history, experience, thought or even 'existence' in such a way that his revelation of himself becomes a relational state. There is no denial of God's relation to man, but its actualism is so pronounced and critical that at no point does it become a 'given' or 'nexus' or 'relational state' which would justify us in speaking about man's relation to God" (1956: 113). "Positively expressed, this means that the relationship of God to man is wholly grounded in God" (1956: 115).

Frei's interpretation of Barth is that the relation of God and the human is a relation between humanity and its judge. Furthermore, Frei agrees with H. Richard Niebuhr that God confronts the human as a judge and even as an enemy of the human's sinful efforts to reach God. "[I]t is quite apparent that the restlessness which underlies Niebuhr's continuous dialectic and necessitates it is due to the fact that in and through all other relations man is fundamentally related to an ultimate 'Other' who confronts him at once as the haunting enemy of his natural religion and as the bestower of grace" (Frei 1975: 66). Thus, for Frei the relationship of God and humanity is grounded in God, and God's relation to us is a judgment rather than an affirmation of human efforts.

Frei sums up what he discovers in Barth by suggesting that Barth's understanding of revelation can be characterized in four ways: as objective, christocentric, immediate, and rooted in the freedom of God (Frei 1956: 458). The first characteristic, the objectivity of God's revelation, is a direct challenge to the understanding that revelation is relational. By "objective," Frei refers to the fact that the act of revelation is grounded in God alone and as such cannot be considered in any way an anthropological datum. "Thus, [God] in his objectivity relates neither mechanically (or externally) nor organically (or internally) to his creatures" (1956: 207). The objectivity of God is founded on the Word of God alone (1956: 457). "This objectivity [in theology] would confess God to be not an object, but an abiding subject who is always the presupposition of thought and action and never encompassed by them. God is objective in the sense of being over against us and never contained within a relation of thought or consciousness to us" (1956: 206).

The second characteristic of revelation is that it is christocentric, in that the centre of revelation is Jesus himself and not his teachings nor how they relate to or affect us. Christ — and not the dynamics of human religion — is the proper focus of the divine-human relationship, since in him nature and grace are related and congruent (Frei 1956: 433). "In him [Jesus Christ] — and in him alone — the concrete and the universal, Bible and transcendental philosophy, immediacy of divine action and indirectness of human knowledge, the object of knowledge and the way of knowledge, the eternal and the temporal are united" (1956: 461).

The third characteristic of revelation is immediacy. Frei uses this concept to denote that God is the free subject of the act of revelation and not the human. In other words, in the event of revelation, it is God who creates the conditions for the reception and understanding of revelation. Revelation is not mediated through human categories of experience or reason, and it is not dependent on human freedom. He writes: "Barth insists that the nature of God's self-revelation is God's freedom in and through his self-communication and over the recipient mode, in man, of this communication" (Frei 1956: 458).

Hence, the fourth characteristic of revelation is that it is rooted in God's freedom and aseity.

1.3 Revelation and biblical Hermeneutics

How does Frei's particular understanding of revelation relate to his understanding and reading of his biblical narrative?

Frei advances on Barth in the following way. Since Scripture is the only witness to revelation, it follows that Scripture, or more precisely the meaning of Scripture, will have similar characteristics to those of revelation. In other words, the characteristics that Barth attributes to revelation Frei tends to attribute to the meaning of the Bible as the only witness to revelation, so that the meaning of the biblical narrative is objective, christocentric, immediate, and rooted in the freedom of God. I will expand this point in the next chapter.

The above advance will be Frei's critique of what he calls "revelation faith." For, according to Frei, there always exists in "revelation faith" the danger of making revelation relational. Relational revelation in turn views the biblical narrative as no more than the record of the initial experience of the disciples, whose meaning is to be understood in that light. In *The Eclipse of biblical Narrative*, Frei critiques German Protestant theology, saying: "Emmanuel Hirsch rightly says that with Baumgarten, 'German Protestant theology moved into the decisive stage of transition from a Bible faith to a revelation faith, for which the Bible is essentially nothing but the specific, given document of revelation'" (1974: 91). Frei's project can be described as an attempt to return to "biblical faith" without a return to the pre-Enlightenment way of reading the Bible. The return to "biblical faith," according to Frei, is accomplished by a "literal" reading of the Bible which corresponds with the previously outlined characteristics of revelation. This is the theme of the following chapter.

2

BIBLICAL HERMENEUTICS

2.1 The Genesis of biblical Hermeneutics

Before discussing what is meant by the "literal meaning" and the "narrative" reading of the Bible that Frei suggests, it is important to identify the problems that Frei believes have affected the way the Bible is read as a result of the question of where revelation is to be located. The polarization between the fact *that* Jesus appeared and *what* Jesus taught was by Frei's account further translated into the search for meaning and thus the rise of hermeneutical theory. This "polarization between hermeneutical extremes, corresponding to the theological affirmation and denial of the positivity of revelation, went like this then: on the one side stood those who affirmed the identity of the real and the intended meanings of the narratives, i.e., their literal meanings and also their historical reliability. On the other side stood those who claimed that the narratives, though literally intended, were as fully historically conditioned as other ancient manuscripts, and that their real meaning, therefore, is not the same as the authors' (literal) intention" (Frei 1974: 64). In other words, the shift from the understanding of revelation as the fact *that* Jesus Christ came to *what* Jesus taught was accompanied by a shift in the understanding of where the meaning of the biblical narrative resides. Different ways of reading the Bible were thus necessitated by different accounts of the location of the meaning of the Bible. For Frei, it is this that gave rise to the hermeneutical problem. The search for *what* Jesus taught posited the meaning of the narrative outside the narrative, whether in historical facts, in the intention of the author, in the Bible's application to life or in ideas. This search for meaning gave rise to the hermeneutical method. On the other hand, if revelation is located in the fact *that* Jesus Christ came, then meaning resides, according to Frei, in the narrative itself, and the appropriate reading of the Bible is then a "literal" reading.

Moreover, these different accounts of the location of the meaning of the Bible and the question of the positivity of revelation were bound up with the division between "meaning" on the one hand and "truth" on the other, and between "meaning" on the one hand and "significance" and "sense" on the other.

2.1.1 The Split Between Meaning and Truth

Frei identifies the split between meaning and truth, and meaning and sense as another aspect of the rise of the hermeneutical problem and the subsequent search for meaning outside the narrative. According to Frei, in the time preceding the Enlightenment, truth and meaning were identical: "In a precritical era, in which literal explicative sense was identical with actual historical reference, literal and figurative reading, far from contradicting each other, belonged together by family resemblance and by need for mutual supplementation. Later on, when explication and reference became separated, the two kinds of readings would not only separate but clash" (Frei 1974: 28). According to Frei, until the Enlightenment the term "meaning" was coincident with the plain sense of the text: the text means what it says. That is, "narrative meaning [which] is identical with the dynamics of its descriptive shape—for which the characters, their social context, the circumstances or incidents, and the theme or themes are all interdependent—was as impossible for Schleiermacher's hermeneutics of understanding as that same outlook had been for the earlier hermeneutical writers" (1974: 312). Over the course of the eighteenth century, 'meaning' came to be understood differently, as it came to refer to the significance of the text for the reader. "Meaning" is no longer an ingredient within the text but involves the response of the reader as one of its aspects. Frei writes: "Where 'meaning' hovers between the explicative sense of a work and its significance for somebody, application becomes an important part of hermeneutics. Precisely this ambiguity, together with the sense of present location and of the difference between then and now, was developed in the hermeneutics of understanding" (1974: 304).

The next question is the issue of "truth" and its relationship to the referential function of the text. In Enlightenment hermeneutics, "truth" was defined in terms of historical factuality: the truth of the text established as the factuality of that to which it purports to refer is verified by historical-critical method. Frei suggests that, while it is appropriate to connect the issue of "referent" to "truth," one must redefine what one means by "referent," especially in the biblical narrative. For Frei, the "referent" of the biblical narrative is the witness to the Word of God. If that is the case, then "truth" is no longer understood in terms of historical factuality but rather in terms of the adequacy and sufficiency of the text for the task of witnessing. Crucially, Frei proposes that it is the grace of God that allows language to be adequate and sufficient. He writes: "And so it is I think rightly proposed that [the reformers] also implied that the text is 'witness' to the Word of God and that its authority derives from that witness rather than from any inherent divinized quality. And is that Word which is witnessed to, is that not the truth . . .? The textual world as witness to the Word of God is not identical with the latter, and yet by the Spirit's grace, it is 'sufficient' for the witnessing" (1993: 163-64). Hunsinger clarifies this point:

> Frei's position on the relation of meaning and truth in the gospel is very subtle and complex....Perhaps one way to bring out what Frei actually affirms would be to put the question like this: if the gospel narratives mean what Frei thinks they mean, then what grounds would be logically appropriate on which to affirm their truth? The meaning of

> the narratives, according to Frei, is their depiction of the
> identity of Jesus Christ. Jesus is depicted as the savior. He is
> depicted as the one who so obeyed God and who so loved
> the guilty in their distress that he voluntarily and vicari-
> ously enacted their salvation. . . . Something like this is what
> Frei takes to be the "fact claim" or meaning of the Gospel
> narratives. This fact claim is neither simple nor simply "his-
> torical". It follows that the grounds on which it would be
> appropriate to affirm the truth of this claim will be as
> unique and mysterious as the claim itself." (1993: 256-66)

The question of "truth" for Frei is connected not so much with
historical factuality as with the adequacy of biblical language to
witness to the Word of God, which at the same time guarantees
the language's adequacy.

In summary, then, the Enlightenment's questions regarding
the positivity of revelation, namely the questions of its factuality
and credibility, when applied to the Bible as the witness to revelation, became questions of truth and meaning. The question of
the truth of the Bible corresponds to that of the factuality of revelation since truth becomes understood as a historical fact: if it
occurred, then it is true. The question of the meaning of the Bible
corresponds to that of the credibility of revelation. "The
hermeneutical polarity concerning biblical narratives, corre-
spond[ed] to, and [was] largely occasioned by, the issue of the
positivity of revelation. The mediating positions tended to be
pushed either toward a specific, ostensive, or referential interpretation, i.e., the affirmation of biblical literalism and the factual reliability of the accounts, or toward a completely historical,
nonostensive understanding of the narratives" (Frei 1974: 255).
As a result, the question of the credibility of revelation and the
meaning of the Bible became the project of apologetic theology.
The project of apologetic theology, according to Frei, is to explain
and make credible the Christian message.

The split between truth and meaning resulted in the belief
that meaning no longer was located in the Bible but rather had

become a question of reference to some location outside the text: What do those narratives in the Bible mean or to what do they refer? Meaning came to be located outside Scripture, and was other than the Bible's literal sense.

2.1.2 The Meaning of the Bible

Frei outlines three possibilities for the location of the meaning of the Bible now that it was no longer considered literal, i.e., it was no longer in the Bible itself. The first possibility is that of empiricism. Thus, Frei writes: "There were . . . those who believed that the subject matter must be ostensive, i.e., the meaning of the narratives is the state of affairs in the spatiotemporal world to which they refer" (1974: 256). For those who held this position meaning, became equated with actual historical reference. As a result, the truth of the narrative was measured by historical criteria, since truth was equated with factuality (1974: 78-85).

Second, there were the rationalists who rejected the idea that the subject matter was an ostensive reference to supposed historical facts. "For them, the subject of the narratives consisted of the ideas or moral and religious truths (*Gehalt*) stated in them in narrative form. We may call them allegorists or rationalists. They believed that the narratives refer ideally rather than ostensively" (Frei 1974: 261). These interpreters believed that the meaning of the Bible consisted of religious or moral truths. Some held that these truths could not be separated from the intention of the author, and thus read the narrative as an allegory. Others, notably Kant, believed that these ideas were represented by the story and had to be understood by interpreting the Bible through reason rather than allegorically. These truths to be found in the text were moral imperatives. "For Kant the meaning of the Biblical narratives was strictly a matter of understanding the ideas they represent in story form. Any historiographical considerations are strictly irrelevant to the interpretation of the subject matter, which is the foundation and advancement of a pure moral disposition in the inner man and its connection with the ideal realm of ends" (Frei 1974: 262).

A third group whom Frei calls "mythophiles" rejected the
notion that the subject matter of the Bible was either ostensive
reference or reference to ideas or truths. For them, "their main
emphasis was to see the subject matter of biblical narratives neither in the events to which they referred nor in the ideas suppos-
edly stated in them in narrative form, but in the consciousness
they represented" (Frei 1974: 265). Frei calls those who held this
position the "mediating thinkers," such as Schleiermacher,
Bultmann, Rahner and others (1974: 128). They believed that religious meaningfulness is not a unique class that stands by itself,
but belongs to a wider frame of meaning and draws its meaningfulness from being related to the general world of human experience. The receiver of revelation or the reader of the Bible is thus
of crucial importance, for without them neither revelation nor the
Bible has meaning. "There is no such thing as revelation without
someone to receive it, and receive it, moreover, as a significant
answer to or illumination of general life questions" (Frei 1974:
129). The subject matter of the Bible concerns human reality.
Thus, the narratives and the events must be understood symbolically. "The triumph and increasing dominance of the mythical
school was due to its making a credible proposal for bridging the
gap between words and meaning, and showing how the texts
mean if they are neither ostensive nor yet allegorical. The connection between the narrative form and the consciousness represented by it (which is their meaning) is made by the device of historical understanding, using the genetic-psychological category
of myth in order to show the distinct consciousness of which
myth is a product" (Frei 1974: 269).

The last two groups, namely the rationalists and the
mythophiles, moreover, saw the meaningfulness of the Bible and
revelation in its application, rather than simply in its explana-
tion. There is, as it were, an imperative to act; the meaning of the
Bible is praxis-oriented. Thus, meaning is "applicative" rather
than being only "explicative." The idealist held that meaning
that is either religious or moral truth must effect a change in

human life. The mythophile likewise saw meaning as it is related to human experience, so that application constitutes part of meaning. "The principle of general hermeneutics for [mediating thinkers'] *applicative* interpretation is the full or partial pertinence of mankind's general religious and moral experience to the Biblical narratives at issue" (Frei 1974: 128).

In summary, in an attempt to locate the positivity of revelation, a further bifurcation between meaning, reference and truth occurred which then gave birth to the problem of interpretation. Frei moves from his historical analysis to suggest a different understanding of meaning that is neither ostensive, idealistic nor symbolic of human consciousness, namely that of "literal meaning."

2.2 Narrative Meaning as the Literal Sense of the Bible

Frei uses different terms in connection with the reading of the Bible: "narrative reading," "figural interpretation," "literal sense," "religious meaning" and "reference." All are important to Frei's enterprise.

However, since Frei uses the categories derived from the literary theory of Erich Auerbach, it may be helpful to outline those categories, even if briefly, especially those that Auerbach applies specifically to the biblical narrative (Auerbach 1953). Auerbach believes that the biblical narrative has an absolute claim to truth. The biblical truth, however, is not a historical truth: "The Biblical narrator was obliged to write exactly what his belief in the truth of the tradition . . . demanded of him. . . . What he produced, then, was not primarily oriented toward 'realism' . . . ; it was oriented toward truth" (Auerbach 1953: 14). Secondly, the biblical narrative seeks to subject our world to its own world, and not the other way around: "The Scripture stories do not, like Homer's, court our favor, they do not flatter us that they may please us and enchant us — they seek to subject us, and if we refuse to be subjected, we are rebels" (1953: 15). Thirdly, the biblical narrative has to be interpreted figuratively: "Figural interpretation establishes a connection between two events or persons in such a way that the first signifies not only itself but also the second, while the second involves or fulfils the first" (1953: 73). Figural interpretation, however, is not simply an interpretation of literary works, but is primarily an interpretation of history and reality. It is an attempt to bring meaning to history (ibid.). "This type of interpretation [figural interpretation] introduces an entirely new and alien element into the antique conception of history . . . a connection is established between two events which are linked neither temporally nor causally—a connection which it is impossible to establish by reason in the horizontal dimension (if I may be permitted to use this term for a temporal extension). It can be established only if both occurrences are vertically linked to Divine Providence, which alone is able to devise such a plan of history and supply the key to its understanding" (1953: 73-74). Furthermore, historically, figural interpretation was defended against the allegorical interpretation where the "basic historical reality of figures" was also defended: "The Church Fathers, especially Tertullian, Jerome, and Augustine, had successfully defended figural realism, that is, the maintenance of the basic historical reality of figures, against all attempts at spiritually allegorical interpretation" (1953: 196).

Thus, fourthly, Auerbach believes that figural interpretation assumes a realistic narrative. In other words, figural interpretation and realistic narrative are intrinsically linked: "A figural schema permits both its poles—the figure and its fulfilment—to retain the characteristics of concrete historical reality, in contradistinction to what obtains with symbolic or allegorical personifications, so that figure and fulfilment—although the one 'signifies' the other—have a significance which is not incompatible with their being real. An event taken as a figure preserves its literal and historical meaning. It remains an event, does not become a mere sign" (Auerbach 1953: 195-96). Finally, Auerbach believes that a literary text must be treated not only as a unit but also as a finished or a closed product.

Auerbach also stressed the importance of narrative by the very fact that in *Mimesis* he analyzed only narrative novels, where he undertook primarily analysis of character.

2.2.1 The Literal Sense of the Bible

Frei suggests that there are different ways of understanding what is meant by literal sense or *sensus literalis*. First, "sensus literalis may describe the precise or fit enactment of the intention to say what comes to be in the text. The intention may be that of the human author. . . . Or it may be the intention of the divine 'author' or 'inspirator'" (Frei 1993: 102). Literal sense, that is, could refer to the intention of the author, which it is the task of the exegetical project to uncover.

According to Frei, literal sense understood as the intention of the author of the text (whether the author is human or divine) has dire effects. It opens the text to historical criticism in one case, or to biblical literalism or fundamentalism in the other. Frei writes: "The appeal to the author's intention had odd effects. On the one hand, it is an encouragement to historical criticism. . . . On the other hand, the text taken as divinely inspired had some devastating effects. . . . The bibliolatry and sheer equation of Bible and doctrine . . . were the logical heirs of this constriction . . . and so were fundamentalist Biblical literalism and factual inerrancy. Both shared a mechanical notion of inspiration" (1993: 102-103). Frei suggests a second use of the expression "literal sense." "Literal sense refers to the descriptive fit between verbum and res, sense and reference, signifier and signified . . . between grammatical/syntactical and conceptual sense, between the narrative sequence and what it renders descriptively. Centrally, in the Christian interpretative tradition of its sacred text, the signifier of the New Testament narrative was taken to be the sequence of the story itself, and what was signified was the identity of the agent cumulatively depicted by it" (1993: 103). Frei endorses the second use of the expression "literal sense" in his earlier writings. The text is not something ostensive, an external expression of the author.

Rather, meaning is identical with the dynamics of the story, that is, with the text's depiction of the way in which the characters interact with each other, and with the situation. In the case of the biblical narrative, the narrative is about Jesus Christ, and thus it follows that the meaning of the story is its depiction of Jesus Christ.

Frei also suggests a third use of "literal sense." "Sensus literalis is the way the text has generally been used in the community. It is the sense of the text in its sociolinguistic context — liturgical, pedagogical, polemical, and so on" (1993: 104). The third use has parallels to the way in which Wittgenstein links meaning and use. The meaning of the text resides in the community's use of it, so that the literal meaning of the biblical narrative is found in the use of Scripture in the corporate life of the Church.[1]

2.2.2 Literal Sense, Meaning and Realistic Narrative

Frei believes that, if literal sense is defined as the way the story proceeds and unfolds, it follows that the "reference" of the story is also its "sense." In other words, if the biblical story is a story depicting Jesus Christ, it follows that the "meaning" of the story is also Jesus Christ. Frei writes: "The meaning of the gospel story for the sensus literalis is, then, that it is *this* story about *this* person as agent and patient, about its surface description and plot" (1993: 112). Frei contrasts his position with that of those who hold that the meaning of the story is in its ostensive reference, whether the reference is to historical occurrence, to ideas, or to a mode-of-being-in-the-world (1993: 117).

What compels Frei to insist on the literal sense of the Bible is his conviction that the biblical writings are best understood as a realistic narrative. He contrasts two ways of viewing the Bible. One way sees the Bible as a witness to the history of salvation; from this viewpoint, the meaning of the Bible is inseparably connected with those reading the Bible, so that meaning becomes a

---

1 It is interesting to note, that, although Frei endorses the second definition of "literal sense," in his later work, he develops it into a definition more similar to that of Lindbeck, namely, the third use of literal sense.

function of interpretation. "The Bible becomes a 'witness' to a history, rather than a narrative text. Its meaning is a unitary complex consisting of the history of saving events, the history of the witnesses' faithful response to them and finally the present faithful stance toward that complex history as a present and future reality . . . its meaning is a function of the temporal sequence of events and interpretive tradition to which the story refers, together with the interpretive stance taken toward this complex sequence" (Frei 1974: 181).

On the other hand, the Bible can be viewed as a realistic narrative. First, the Bible is a *narrative* and, for Frei, it is important to grasp "that a narrative text is its own world, whether it 'refers' in some way or not, and that it should therefore be *read* as a text" (Frei 1990: 155). Second, the Bible is — to use terms Frei borrows from Auerbach — a *realistic* narrative: history-like but not historical; fact-like but not factual (Frei 1974: 16). As such, its meaning cannot be discovered by identifying facts behind the text, since its meaning is not identical with its reference to facts of history. The meaning of a realistic narrative is a function of the narrative itself, that is, of the depiction of the story itself and its unfolding. Frei writes: "In realistic narrative, the meaning of a story is a function of the specific storied representation" (1974: 181). "Narrative meaning is identical with the dynamics of its descriptive shape — for which the characters, their social context, the circumstances or incidents, and the theme or themes are all interdependent" (1974: 312).

Thus, in realistic narrative the meaning of the story coincides with the rendering of the story or its depiction of events; in this way its meaning is its literal sense (Frei 1974: 11).

Frei critiques thinkers such as McFague and Tracy for making sense and truth a function of meaning. Frei makes meaning a function of literal sense and truth. In other words, those thinkers first ascertain the meaningfulness of the biblical story and then from meaning they move on to the questions of truth and sense. Frei, on the other hand, suggests that one must first look at the literal sense having taken truth for granted, since truth is granted by God, and then ask the question of its meaning to us (1993: 163).

It is important to recognize that what Frei refers to as a narrative reading of the Bible is different from what is customarily referred to as narrative theology. A narrative reading of the Bible is textually based, while narrative theology is anthropologically based. Narrative theology works in the realm of hermeneutics and meaning as understanding, while a narrative reading of the Bible is a particular way of reading the Bible where meaning is its literal sense. "The difference between a textually focused inquiry, working with the specificity of the narratives, and a more generally focused one, for which the biblical narratives are an illustration or illumination of 'narrativity' as an elemental aspect of being human and of human experience, is not absolute. But it is important" (Frei 1990: 160).

2.2.3 Figural Interpretation and Literal Sense

Another important term related to a realistic reading of biblical narrative where there is literal sense is "figural interpretation." Simply put, figural interpretation refers to the fact that the hermeneutical principle by which the biblical narrative is understood is the figure of Jesus Christ himself and not our present situation and context. "Figural meaning is part of the specific historical context in which the figure arises, and not a pattern retrospectively applied to the earlier context from the vantage point of a later situation" (Frei 1974: 192). "Figural interpretation . . . is a grasp of a common pattern of occurrence and meaning together, the pattern being dependent on the reality of the unitary temporal sequence which allows all the single narrations within it to become parts of a single narration" (Frei 1974: 34). In the biblical narrative, the "pattern of occurrence" through which the narrative is unified and finds meaning is the figure of Jesus Christ. In other words, figural interpretation is an expression of a christocentric interpretation of the Bible, "so that not only 'Old Testament' narrative but its legal texts and its prophetic as well as wisdom literature are taken to point beyond themselves to their 'fulfilment' in the 'New Testament.' The Jewish texts are taken as 'types' of the story of Jesus as their common 'antitype'" (Frei 1993: 120).

By now, it should be clear why literal sense, figural interpretation and narrative reading go together. A realistic narrative reading of the biblical story about Jesus Christ finds the story's meaning in the actual events concerning the character Jesus Christ. Moreover, Jesus Christ as the ascriptive subject of the narrative illumines and unifies the biblical story.

> The creed, "rule of faith" or "rule of truth" which governed the Gospels' use in the church asserted the primacy of their literal sense. Moreover, it did this right from the beginning in the ascriptive even more than the descriptive mode. That "Jesus" — not someone else or nobody in particular — is the subject, the agent, and patient of these stories is said to be their crucial point, and the descriptions of events, sayings, personal qualities, and so forth, become literal by being firmly predicated of him. (Frei 1993: 123)

Clearly, such a proposal raises again the question of reference. The question falls into two parts: First, can religious and biblical language refer and, second, if religious and biblical language refer, to what do they refer? Both parts of the question concern the realism of language.

In answering the first part of the question, Frei suggests that "we can affirm that in the Christian confession of divine grace, the truth is such that the text is sufficient. There is a fit due to the mystery of grace between truth and text" (1993: 166).[2] But if religious and biblical language refer, to what do they refer? Frei does not agree with the literalists, idealists, empiricists or mythophiles that religious language has an ostensive reference, that it refers to either historical facts, ideas, or the experiences of

---

2 Here, Frei is close to Barth. See, for example, Hunsinger 1987: 209-23.

disciples or that it is symbolic of our own human reality. To what, then, does it refer? Hunsinger puts it aptly: "Frei is not claiming that the gospel narratives make no ostensive reference. He is rather claiming that they make no ostensive reference to an object to which we have independent epistemic access and whose factuality can be affirmed on any grounds other than faith. In other words, he is claiming that they make ostensive reference to the mystery of the presence of Jesus Christ, the risen savior, whose identity as such they depict" (1993: 266). In other words, literal sense, meaning and truth, and reference all coincide because they concern the mystery of Jesus Christ, whose presence is approximately affirmed in faith.

2.2.4 Frei's Later Development of Literal Sense

In his later work, notably his article "The 'Literal Reading' of Biblical Narrative in Christian Tradition: Will it Stretch or Will it Break?," Frei develops further his understanding of the literal sense of the biblical narrative. Here, he does not maintain the strict difference between the second and third definitions of the literal sense, i.e., the literal sense as textually based and the literal sense as communally based. Thus, the literal sense is not only understood according to the second definition as "the descriptive fit between sense and reference, the sequence of the story and the identity of the agent," but also can include the third definition. Frei writes:

> What of the future of the "literal reading"? The less entangled in theory and the more firmly rooted not in a narrative (literary) tradition but in its primary and original context, a religious community's "rule" for faithful reading, the more clearly it is likely to come into view....From that perspective, a theory confined to describing how and in what specific kind of context a certain kind of reading functions is an improvement over the kind of theoretical endeavor that tries to justify its very possibility in general. (1993: 139)

In one way, Frei's most basic tenets about revelation, figural interpretation, truth and reference have not changed dramatically in this later essay. However, some development in his understanding of literal sense has occurred, in that it is related not only to the textual realities of realistic narrative, but also to the community's consensus on how the text is to be read.

2.3 Literal Sense and the Doctrine of Revelation

In summary, Frei suggests a different way of reading the Bible, a reading that is in accordance with the understanding of revelation he finds in Barth. Frei understands the Gospel stories as realistic narratives to be read as such, for "in realistic narrative, the meaning of a story is a function of the specific storied representation" (1974: 181). The meaning of the narrative resides on the *surface* of the text, not in ostensive reference, nor in the intention of the author, nor in religious or moral truths. Meaning does not reside *behind* the text, nor is it discovered by attention to something other than the narrative itself. Meaning is not generated by the subject who reads the text: in this way, meaning does not reside *in front* of the text. This realistic narrative reading "represents a turn away from the subject, from the whole Kantian and post-Kantian scheme that the Christ of faith is what he is to the extent that he is it to our faith, that 'meaning' is always 'meaning' in relation to 'understanding,' to a subjective process or inner event" (Frei 1992: 85). The meaning of the text is autonomous, in that the text is a semiotic world of its own, whose meaning is not dependent on the recipient (ibid.).

This narrative reading of the Bible does not, however, represent a return to a naive pre-Enlightenment reading of the Bible. First, over against the pre-Enlightenment equating of literal or figurative sense with historical factuality, the literal sense of realistic narrative is not coincident with historical factuality (Frei 1974: 16). Secondly, even in the literal reading there is no return to the pre-critical stance, where the subject has absolutely nothing to do with the interpretive process and its results. But "the irreducibly personal element comes only in the 're-presented' 'disclosure' situation, that is in 'understanding' appropriation of the text" (Frei 1993: 128). The Bible has its own world as it were; the reader's task is to fit into that world rather than locate the text within the reader's own subjectivity. Frei writes: "Biblical interpretation became an imperative need, but its direction was that of incorporating extra-Biblical thought, experience, and reality into the one real world detailed and made accessible by the Biblical story—not the reverse" (1974: 3).

The most important characteristic of the narrative reading is that its dynamic is descriptive or ascriptive rather than explicative or applicative. In reading the Bible and theologizing about it, one is to be engaged in *redescribing* events rather than in *explaining* why or how these events took place. To engage in explaining is to undertake the quest for criteria and thus, to get involved in apologetic theology (Frei 1992: 81). On the other hand, "the theoretical task compatible with the literal reading of the Gospel narratives is that of describing how and in what context it functions" (Frei 1993: 144).

By now, it should be evident that narrative reading of the Bible, as defined by Christians, accords with an understanding of revelation as located in the fact *that* Jesus Christ came rather than in *what* he said. For the meaning of the fact *that* Jesus Christ came is not dependent upon whether the subject understands or receives Jesus Christ; rather, it is in the event itself. Thus, to speak about that event is to describe it, rather than to develop arguments in favour of it. Revelation according to Frei's interpretation of Barth, is objective, christocentric, immediate and reflects the freedom and aseity of God. Similarly, for Frei, the meaning of the Bible as a witness to revelation has to be objective, christocentric, immediate and has to reflect the freedom of God. Because the meaning of the biblical narrative is "autonomous," residing on the surface of the text apart from the reader, the meaning of the narrative is *objective*. Secondly, the biblical narrative concerns Jesus Christ; its meaning does not reside in the intention of the author, or in historical events or moral truths, nor is it symbolic of the wider human reality. This makes the meaning of the Bible *christocentric*. Thirdly, the world of the Bible is the world that encompasses the world of the reader and not the other way around. In the act of reading, it is God who reveals and judges the reader's life and achievements. Meaning is *not mediated* by the activities of the reader. Finally, since the meaning of the narrative does not depend on the recipient or the reader and is not conditioned by it, God's *freedom* and lordship is thus safeguarded.

2.4 The Theological Task

In the light of these proposals about biblical interpretation, what is the role of theology? Frei explains: "I believe that it is not the business of Christian theology to argue the possibility of Christian truth any more than the instantiation or actuality of that truth. . . . Hence, I should want to draw a sharp distinction between the logical structure as well as the content of Christian belief, which it is the business of theologians to describe but not to explain or argue, and the totally different logic of how one comes to believe, or the possibility of believing immanent in human existence" (1993: 30). Theology is to be confessional rather than apologetic (Frei 1974: xi); its task is to redescribe Christian assertions, not to explain them or discuss the possibility of their truth. For the truth of Christian revelation is something that is attributed to God and not dependent on its recipient. The truth of Christian claim is a "matter of divine, self-authenticating action and revelation" (Frei 1993: 30).

As to the role of theology in relation to the biblical text, theology must answer the question: "What does this narrative say or mean, never mind whether it can become a meaningful possibility of life perspective for us or not?" (Frei 1993: 40). Theology has to find and describe the literal sense of the biblical narrative. The role of theology as confessional and descriptive is in line with the task of a narrative reading of the Bible and the search for its literal sense. It is also consistent with Frei's move away from relational revelation. The apologetic agenda attempts to show the meaningfulness and credibility of Christianity with reference to a wider world of meaning. It further attempts to show the relationship between the human quest for meaning and divine grace. Hunsinger puts it aptly: "[Frei] had initially criticized 'modern liberal theology' as a whole for replacing christology with anthropology and for thereby disregarding the hermeneutical significance of the gospel narratives" (1993: 262). Thus, in the final analysis apologetic theology does not speak of God but is reduced to speaking of the human. Theology is reduced to anthropology. In Frei's opinion, that is what happens when the interest of theology is centred around *what* Jesus Christ taught and meant, for by its very definition it includes a *why*. Thus, theology becomes involved in explicative and applicative work rather than descriptive work.

3

JESUS THE CHRIST

It is important to note how a particular doctrine of revelation determines a particular way of reading the Bible and seeking meaning, which in turn determines a particular way of theologizing, in this case expounding a christology. For Frei, theology is a confessional rather than an apologetic enterprise. That is, the role of theology is to describe assertions of Christian faith rather than to seek to establish reasons for their reasonableness or conditions for their intelligibility. The role of theology is descriptive or ascriptive rather than explicative or applicative. Frei's opinion on the role of theology is illustrated in the way in which he poses the question concerning the identity of Jesus Christ and in his answer to that question.

Frei proposes that the question concerning Jesus Christ's identity must be a "formal" question (Frei 1967: 89). A formal question about Jesus Christ or the narrative is a question whose answer does not overwhelm the person or the story. One can pose the question about Jesus Christ in such a way that its wealth of content overwhelms the possible answer and thus hinders the answer's emergence from the narrative. Conversely, a formal question is loose and flexible enough to allow the answer to the question to emerge unencumbered. A formal question is a "contentless" question which allows the content to be supplied by the answer that emerges from the narrative. This is in contrast to two other ways of posing the question about Jesus Christ that are not formal in character (Frei 1967: 90). One such question about Jesus Christ would be "How does the person of Jesus in the Biblical narrative relate and illuminate our contemporary existence?" In this kind of question, the person in the story becomes of secondary importance. Primary importance goes to the question itself, which inquires into the person's relationship to us. Frei finds this approach in the theologies of Bultmann and Tillich (1967: 89). The other kind of question about Jesus Christ seeks to add supposed depth and dimension to the person in the story by looking to sources other than the story itself. This approach again overwhelms the person of the story. Thus, "the category of identity serves more than a formal function, for it gives independent content to Jesus' person or character, which then shapes the reading of the story. (There are innumerable instances of this procedure in modern theology. One that raised considerable interest in scholarly circles some years ago is James M. Robinson's *A New Quest of the Historical Jesus*" (1967: 90).

Clearly, these kinds of questions fit the different answers to the positivity of revelation and the resultant quest for meaning. The "formal" question sees the meaning of revelation as an ingredient within the narrative. The second kind of question sees meaning in relation to human existence, and thus emphasizes the importance of hermeneutics. The third kind of question sees meaning in the historical quest for Jesus, and thus emphasizes the importance of the historical—critical method. According to Frei, the "formal" question of who and what Jesus is like, according to the narrative, is the appropriate christological procedure.

In answering the questions of who Jesus is and what he is like, Frei makes two moves to counter what he perceives to be the inadequacies of apologetic christology.

In the first move, Frei uses categories derived from the literary theory of Erich Auerbach and the philosophical anthropology of Gilbert Ryle (Frei 1974: vii). The question of what Jesus is like will be answered by what he calls intention-action description, and who Jesus is will be answered by what he calls self-manifestation description (Frei 1967: 91). "Intention-action description" and "self-manifestation description" are terms borrowed from Ryle. The claim is, that who a person is *is* his or her actions. In other words, "the styles and procedures of people's activities are the way their minds work and are not merely imperfect reflections of postulated secret processes which were supposed to be the workings of the mind. . . . Overt intelligent performances are not clues to the workings of minds; they are those workings" (Ryle 1949: 58). Thus, to know the identity of someone, one does not go "behind" the actions to seek an intention that acts as the cause for actions by which the person can be known. In other words, one does not seek the "ghost-in-the-machine" (1949: 32). One simply observes what people do, and what they do is who they are. That applies equally to Jesus. To know who Jesus is one observes his actions. However, the only place one can find about the actions of Jesus Christ is the biblical narrative. In other words, only in the biblical narrative is the identity of Jesus Christ known.

Frei's second move is that, in answering the question about Jesus in terms of his actions as manifested in the biblical narrative, he opts to start with what he terms the identity of Jesus, rather than his meaningfulness to or presence to us today. We will return to this later.

3.1 Christ's Relationship to Christians

According to Frei, there are two possibilities for answering the question of who Jesus is. One option is to start with the relationship of Christ to Christians (Frei 1967: 1). In other words, one starts with how Jesus is present to us, and then one moves on to answer the question of his identity. In this approach, Jesus' saving works in regard to us become our primary point of departure. It is not the actions of Jesus in the biblical narrative that constitute our departure point, but Jesus as he encounters us in our experience, so that the identity of Jesus is defined in relation to us, rather than being defined strictly by the biblical narrative. According to this model, we move from Christian experience towards christology.

Frei, by contrast, seeks to start with Jesus' own identity as presented in the biblical narrative, and only later moves on to answer the question of how Jesus relates to us. In this second option, christology becomes the basis for all other doctrines.

As we have seen, Frei's critique of the apologetic agenda is that it has always started with the question of how Jesus is present and related to us. However, he suggests that there are many problems associated with such a start. He writes: "We noted first, that there is no precise parallel between the presence of Jesus Christ and the way we think of the presence of other persons and, secondly, that the use of imagination in regard to Jesus cannot adequately represent his presence to us as the resurrected Lord" (1967: 36). The result of using our imagination in the attempt to understand what it means that Jesus is present to us is that we are forced to understand the life, death and resurrection of Jesus symbolically rather than literally, because we have no precedent in our experience for such a presence. The result of starting with the category of presence is that the presence of Jesus Christ becomes another aspect of our own reality. "His conception, birth, life, death, resurrection, and ascension become, in this view, poetic expressions of a dimension of our own existence that belongs to no literal time and place, but to the common ground and horizon of man's true spirit — veiled from sight, but no less real for that" (Frei 1967: 32). Jesus' presence becomes so connected with our own self-presence that "his presence is not his own; indeed, he is diffused into humanity by becoming one with it. And we, in turn, find in him the mysterious symbol expressing our own ultimate lack of abiding presence and identity" (1967: 86).

3.2 Christ's Presence to Self: His Identity

In contrast with this, Frei suggests that we should start with the identity of Jesus Christ when discussing him, for it is only in starting with Jesus' identity that we will make sense of Jesus' presence. What does Frei mean by Jesus' identity?

Frei recognizes that the category "identity," like the concept of time, is difficult to define since its meaning and use involve reference to itself, rather than to some ostensive "thing" (Frei 1993: 59). However, he gives the following "loose" definition or formal description of the term "identity": "Identity is essentially the action and testimony of a personal being by which he lays true claim to being himself and the same at an important point as well as over a length of time" (1993: 60). The term "identity" is closely related to that of "ascriptive subject," and it is described in intention-action and self-manifestation categories (1993: 74). Explication of these categories will further our understanding of the term "identity."

The ascriptive subject is the "I" which is the subject of all actions or, in other words, the "I" to which is ascribed the predicate of a sentence. Frei speaks of "[the] "I", the 'index word' Ryle calls it, which serves to indicate that to which both states of consciousness and physical characteristics are ascribed, the ascriptive centre or focus of intentional activity" (1993: 64). Frei holds that this "I" is ultimate, in that qualities and characteristics are predicated on it, without the "I" referring to anything other than itself. The "I" is also elusive, to be likened to Kant's "elusive noumena." The self must be silent about one performance and that is itself. Finally, the "I" is persistent through time (ibid.). Because of all the above, the "I" can be described only indirectly.

Because the "I" can be described only indirectly, the categories Frei uses for its description are those of intention-action and self-manifestation. The intention-action description is a way of looking at intentions not so much as causes of actions as reasons for actions. Here, Frei recalls Ryle's distinction between "cause" and "reason."

To explain his distinction between "cause" and "reason," Ryle offers the example of a glass having been broken. If one asks the question why it broke, two answers could be given: because a stone hit it, or because it was brittle. According to Ryle, the first answer is the correct one, for the stone hitting the glass is the "cause" of the breakage: it is an event, it takes place in a specific time and space. However, if the brittleness of the glass is seen as the "cause" of the breakage, a category mistake is made. The brittleness of the glass is a "dispositional adjective" and not a "cause"; it describes the disposition of the glass which, upon being hit by a stone, shatters. The dispositional adjective is more like a "reason." Thus, one can say: The glass has a disposition of being brittle, so that when it is hit by a stone it breaks. In Ryle's words:

> There are at least two quite different senses in which an occurrence is said to be "explained"; and there are correspondingly at least two quite different senses in which we ask "why." . . . The first sense is the causal sense. To ask why the glass broke is to ask what caused it to break, and we explain, in this sense, the fracture of the glass when we report that a stone hit it. The "because" clause in the explanation reports an event, namely the event which stood to the fracture of the glass as cause to effect. . . . But very frequently we look for and get explanations of occurrences in another sense of "explanation." We ask why the glass shivered when struck by the stone and we get the answer that it was because the glass was brittle. Now "brittle" is a dispositional adjective; that is to say, to describe the glass as brittle is to assert a general hypothetical proposition about the glass . . . the "because" clause does not report a happening or a cause; it states a law-like proposition. People commonly say of explanations of this second kind that they give the "reason" for the glass breaking when struck. (1949: 86)

Ryle's logic could be applied to the human situation: when one says a man boasts when he is in the company of another, it means that the "reason" for his boast is vanity; however, the "cause" of his boast is meeting the other person (Ryle 1949: 89).

"Reason" and "cause" thus describe two different realities. They do not represent a breach of logical rules. "Reasons" are dispositional adjectives, while "causes" are events; they are episodic. Thus, words like "'know,' 'believe,' 'aspire,' 'clever' and 'humorous' are determinable dispositional words. They signify abilities, tendencies or proneness to do; not things of one unique kind, but things of lots of different kinds" (Ryle 1949: 118).

This brings us to another very important point: some dispositional adjectives such as "intelligent," "kind," "proud" and so on are not single-track dispositions; they are multi-track dispositions. "There are many dispositions the actualizations of which can take a wide and perhaps unlimited variety of shapes" (Ryle 1949: 44). "Intelligent capacities are not single-track dispositions, but are dispositions admitting of a wide variety of more or less dissimilar exercises" (1949: 56). To be prone to smoking is a single-track disposition because this disposition has only one manifestation: smoking (1949: 43). However, being intelligent could be manifested in activities such as playing chess, doing mathematics, or dealing with a particular situation. Ryle gives the example of Jane Austen's heroine, Elizabeth Bennett, to describe whose pride the author wrote a narrative in which the heroine's pride was manifested in her words, actions, thoughts and feelings (1949: 44).

Let us return to Frei. If one wishes to describe the identity of Jesus in terms of the intention-action category, one must seek the one characteristic that unifies his identity, i.e., the one multi-track disposition that captures his identity and thus is the reason for the way he is, rather than the cause of his actions. Frei holds that Jesus' perfect obedience to God is the predominant quality of behaviour that was descriptive of all his acts (1967: 102). In other words, obedience is the clue to Jesus' identity. For Frei, this is in contrast to viewing love as the prominent behavioural pattern. However, since Jesus' "obedience to God was one with his intention to do what had to be done on men's behalf . . . his mission was identical with love for men" (1967: 103). The call for obedience to God is fulfilled in loving others, so that the primary quality is obedience and not love. Frei writes: "The *referent* of Jesus' obedience is the will of God and his purpose. . . . The *content* or meaning of that obedience is the pattern of merciful, saving activity" (1967: 111). Thus, what defines Jesus Christ is his relationship to God, which then determines his relationship to us (rather than vice versa). Obedience is the primary characteristic, for it describes Jesus' relationship to God as the obedient Son. Obedience, in turn, is the reason for Jesus' loving actions towards us.

Finally, we come to the category of self-manifestation. Here, Frei seeks those actions of Jesus that truly manifest his identity, since one's action *is* oneself. Frei proposes that there are three stages in the identification of Jesus through his actions in the biblical narrative. In other words, the focusing of Jesus' identity takes place in three stages. "There are in the first place the pre-birth, birth, and infancy stories. The striking fact about this first stage is that both in the story and its liturgical or poetic decorative material the person of Jesus is identified wholly in terms of the identity of a community, the people of Israel" (Frei 1993: 77). According to Frei, the first stage is not the place where Jesus is seen as the unsubstitutable subject. That is because in the first stage the story of Jesus functions as a symbol of Israel. However, "with the account of Jesus' baptism, the story undergoes a break, or rather a decisive transition to a second stage. Far more than in the first part he appears as an agent, an individual in his own right. . . . Nonetheless he retains something of the symbolical or representative quality that he had in the first part of the accounts. But now it is not the part of which he is representative. Instead it is the immediately pending rule of God" (Frei 1993: 78). Only in the second stage does Jesus begin to emerge as a unique person. There are mighty deeds such as feeding the multitude, raising the dead, opening the eyes of the blind and so forth, all of which are signs of the kingdom. However, his unsubstitutable self has not yet fully emerged. "The transition to the third stage comes with Jesus' brief announcement to his disciples that he and they would now go to Jerusalem, and his prediction concerning the Son of Man's fate" (Frei 1993: 79). In the third stage, the identity of Jesus Christ emerges as that of a person who has a specific mission. The identification of Jesus Christ with Israel or the Kingdom of God becomes more difficult. As the story unfolds, we move into the passion and the resurrection of Jesus Christ. They constitute the later part of the third stage. "In terms of the movement that we have traced, from a symbolic or representative person to an individual in his own right, we have reached the last stage of the story. There is no further focusing of his identity. In this respect the passion and resurrection represent, in the very transition from one to the other, not two stages but one. In both, he is equally himself, none other than Jesus of Nazareth. In the unity of this particular transition, passion and resurrection, he is most of all himself, most historical as an individual in his own right" (Frei 1993: 80). Frei interprets the resurrection appearances as the place where Jesus Christ is fully himself. In the resurrection appearances Jesus Christ's unsubstitutable singular identity emerges (Frei 1967: 49). Frei holds that this is the case because in the resurrection appearances Jesus has not only his own identity but also his own presence. In the resurrection Jesus has his own place to which he can withdraw, and then later can appear and share his presence with others. Frei believes that the narrative itself suggests that in the resurrection Jesus becomes his unsubstitutable self. In the third stage, that is, in the resurrection, "he emerged fully as the one unsubstitutable Jesus of Nazareth — and this as much in the resurrection as in the passion" (1967: 136).

Furthermore, in the resurrection the interaction of divine action and human actions takes place. In the resurrection, God's hidden action becomes manifested, so that "in his passion and death the initiative of Jesus disappears more and more into that of God; but in the resurrection, where the initiative of God is finally and decisively climaxed and he alone is and can be active, the sole identity to mark the presence of that activity is Jesus. God remains hidden, and even reference to him is almost altogether lacking. Jesus of Nazareth, he and none other, marks the presence of the action of God" (Frei 1967: 121). Finally, Frei believes that the resurrection unifies the intention-action and self-manifestation of the identity of Jesus Christ as the presence of God (1967: 123).

One final aspect of Frei's argument remains to be considered. Frei believes that Jesus is most historical in the passion and resurrection accounts. He outlines four different ways in which the resurrection accounts have been understood (1993: 201-203). First, there are those who understand the resurrection to be mythical, and thus interpret it symbolically. The resurrection is interpreted existentially, as a way of articulating the change that befalls the disciples' faith and lives. Second, there are those who claim that the biblical narrative is an accurate record of what took place, so that the resurrection is a historical fact that can be verified by historical methods. Third, there are those who hold that the story is about Jesus, and that the resurrection accounts are to be understood spiritually rather than physically. Finally, there are those who believe that the resurrection is historical and factual, in that it is real. However, it is not historical in the way that a statement such as "Queen Victoria died in 1901" is historical. The resurrection is a fact, but not such that it can be verified by historical methods. For if it were so verifiable, the resurrection would become an instance of the wider category of historical facts that can be verified, whereas the resurrection is unique; an instance of itself. The only language that is adequate to describe it is that of miracle. Thus, Frei writes: "Finally, others read the accounts as meaning what they say, so that their subject is indeed the bodily resurrected Jesus. They also believe that a miracle—the miracle of the resurrection in particular—is a real event; however, it is one to which human depiction and conception are inadequate, even though the literal description is the best that can be offered" (1993: 203). This understanding of the resurrection accords with a realistic reading of the biblical narrative, where meaning is the literal sense. The narrative represents an adequate witness to reality rather than an accurate report of it.

To sum up the section on identity:

> We have tried to describe the identity of Jesus in his story by
> means of a formal scheme for identity description. We
> asked, "What was he like?" and answered with an inten-
> tion-action description provided by the narrative, pointing
> us to the crucified savior, the obedient Jesus who enacted
> the good that God intended for men. The enactment of this
> intention came to a climax in the crucifixion-resurrection
> sequence. We also asked, "Who is he?" and answered with
> an identification description provided by the whole Gospel
> in its transitions, pointing us to the unsubstitutable Jesus of
> Nazareth who, as that one man, is the Christ and the pres-
> ence of God. And again, his identity is most transparent in
> the crucifixion-resurrection sequence. (Frei 1967: 137)

How does Frei move from here to the question of Jesus Christ's
presence to the believer or in the community?

3.3 Transition from the Identity to the Presence of Jesus Christ

The final move in Frei's argument is cryptic and not very easy to
discern. He proposes that, once the identity of Jesus Christ is
understood properly, it is inconceivable to perceive his identity
without his presence. Thus, "in short, to speak of the identity of
Jesus, in which he is affirmed by the believer to be present, is also
to speak of the presence of *God*" (Frei 1967: 154). That is to say,
the presence of Jesus Christ to us now is an intrinsic aspect of his
identity, because the identity of Jesus Christ as the revelation of
God is coincident with the presence of God. As the identity of
Jesus becomes more focused, as the narrative moves towards the
resurrection, so does the unsubstitutability of Jesus in full unity
with the presence of God.

To articulate this, Frei speaks of the presence of Jesus Christ
as the Holy Spirit: "When Christian believers speak of the presence of Jesus Christ now — in contrast to his presence at the time
of his earthly life, death, and resurrection, as well as in contrast

to his final presence in the future mode—they use the term 'Spirit' or 'Holy Spirit'" (1967: 155). The Holy Spirit unites Christ's identity with his presence. Furthermore, reference to the Spirit also draws attention to the fact that the presence of Jesus Christ is indirect. This presence must be put in negative form. Thus, "it is the presence of one whose identity is such that he cannot be conceived as not present" (ibid.).

Furthermore, when Christians refer to Christ's presence they refer to the church as the indirect presence of Christ (Frei 1967: 147). Thus, it is possible to speak of Christ's presence in the Sacrament and the Word. This, however, is only possible because the Spirit constitutes the unity of Jesus Christ's identity and presence. Thus, for Frei, Sacrament and Word represent the spatial and temporal manner in which the present mode of Christ's presence is there for the believer (Frei 1967: 164).

3.4 Experience and Theology

We have already noted a development in the thought of Hans Frei. In his earlier work, he holds that the literal sense of the biblical narrative is textually based, in that the literal sense and meaning coincide with and refer to the story of the text. In his later work, there is a development in his understanding of the literal sense of the biblical narrative, which is now perceived not only as textually based but also as involving the community's use and understanding of the text. This development in Frei's understanding of literal sense was accomplished by a development in his understanding of the role of theology. In his earlier work, theology is a matter of redescribing Christian beliefs and the story of Jesus Christ. However, in his later work, with literal meaning also being communally based, theology is about the redescription of the language of the Christian community. This development also reflects a development in his understanding of the place of "experience" in theology.

In his earlier work, there is no place for experience in theology proper. There, Frei sets out three stages of theology: *explica-*

tio, meditatio and *applicatio* (1993: 113). Theology proper involves the first two stages. In the first stage, one retells the story; in the second stage, one uses a conceptual framework to redescribe the story. It is only in the third stage that the story is related to our context, and that a place emerges for "experience," for in an attempt to relate the story to us in the here and now our own "experience" is taken into account. Pastoral theology and ethics fit the third stage. For through pastoral theology and ethics, the theology proper of the first two stages is *applied* to the life of the community. In this scheme there is a unidirectional relationship between the biblical story and our lives. We learn the literal sense of the story, which is objective, and in the second stage apply this understanding to our lives. Frei writes: "Applicatio or use [is] in its own way as inclusive as the second stage. It is the skill to relate the story (for other texts) to the context, the judgment that we do or do not share a world with the text and with the community in which it has functioned since its first telling. The text is meaningful by appropriation, its meaning is performatively or existentially realized" (1993: 113-14). This understanding is in contrast to a more correlational understanding of theology and "experience."

In his later work, Frei adds a communal dimension to his understanding of the literal sense. The literal sense of the biblical narrative is not only what the story says but also how the community understands this story. But how the community understands and uses the story is always in constant dialogue with the community's life. In other words, the life of the community is now the work of theology proper. Theology proper is no longer restricted only to the biblical story as written, but now must engage in the redescription of the community's life.

We must bear in mind, however, that Frei does not use the word "experience." Thus, experience for Frei at no point means an individualistic experience that is understood as uninterpreted or that springs from the depths of the human. For Frei, the experience that he talks about is the Christian community's experience and life. In other words, the expressions that Frei uses are: church, Christian community and, finally, the way the biblical narrative is used. In my opinion, they are another way of talking about experience. To illustrate this, I will return briefly to Frei's concern in his book *The Identity of Jesus Christ.*

To borrow his own language, Frei is concerned with the "identity" of Christians. He observes that, precisely because of the liberal agenda, Christians are losing their "identity." The metaphor that Frei uses is Lindbeck's metaphor of language and culture. Christians are losing their Christian language and culture. Christianity and Christians are disappearing into the wider culture of the Western world. In an ironic parallel, as Christ's "identity" is being lost when our concern is to make him "present" in our time, our "identity" is being lost when our sole concern is our "presence" to our own times, exemplified in our concern for our experience. To recapture Jesus' "identity" and ours we have to let go of the concern for Jesus' "presence" to Christians and our 'presence' to the world in the form of our experience. Frei's Christology, which starts from "identity," is a turning away from the category of experience.

Although Frei's thought has undergone development concerning the understanding of literal sense, theology and experience, his concern remains that of the "identity" of the Christian community. That is, even though Frei may move to a more positive and active role for experience in his later work, it is still the experience of the Christian community that he is interested in, the experience that forms the community's identity. Let us now turn to Schillebeeckx's approach to "experience" in theological method and christology.

PART TWO

EDWARD SCHILLEBEECKX

4

DOCTRINAL CONSIDERATIONS:
THE DOCTRINE OF REVELATION

Before discussing Edward Schillebeeckx's theological position, it may be helpful to mention something about his life and background (Schreiter 1984: 1-4). Schillebeeckx, a Dominican priest, was born in 1914 and raised in Belgium. His early education was by the Jesuits. However, after studying the lives of several founders of religious orders, he decided to enter the Dominican order at the age of nineteen. The charisma of its founder, St. Dominic, seemed to suit his temperament best. During his studies, prior to ordination in 1941, Schillebeeckx studied philosophy under the guidance of the Dominican De Petter. De Petter instructed Schillebeeckx in the philosophies of Kant, Hegel and the phenomenologists; he also instructed him in the study of Freud.

After the Second World War, in 1945, Schillebeeckx went to Paris to do his doctoral work. In Paris, he encountered the theological movement that advocated a return to the "sources" as a method of theological reflection, and rejected dependence on secondary materials such as commentaries and manuals. The two notable figures he encountered in Paris were Yves Congar and Marie-Dominique Chenu. Chenu's insistence on historical research, on the one hand, and commitment to justice on the other had a lasting effect on Schillebeeckx's theology, and he went on to do his doctoral work under the direction of Chenu. In 1947, Schillebeeckx returned to Louvain and finished his doctoral thesis in 1951.

Schillebeeckx stayed in Louvain until 1958; he moved then to Nijmegen, in the Netherlands, to teach at the Catholic University of Nijmegen. While in the Netherlands he became very much involved in the life of the Dutch Church. As a result, Schillebeeckx became an advisor to the Dutch bishops, and in 1960 he assisted them in writing their joint pastoral letter outlining a liberal agenda planned Second Vatican Council.

In the same year, Schillebeeckx travelled to the United States where he came in contact with what are called "secularization" and the "death of God" theologies. He returned to Nijmegen, where he continues his work until the present day.

Precisely because Schillebeeckx is conversant with the philosophical and intellectual currents of his time, his thought has undergone considerable change and development (Schreiter 1984: 19-24). In his earlier work from the 1950s and early 1960s, Schillebeeckx was very much influenced by Thomistic thought. Though he sets aside the Thomistic interpretive framework in his later work, several theological concepts continue to inform his theology. The understanding that God can be known through the mediation of the created world because of "proportionate analogy of being," that is, that the creature shares something of the creator, is the basis of Schillebeeckx's theology of revelation.

In the mid-1960s, Schillebeeckx came in contact with Anglo-American philosophies of language, which prompted his sensitivity to language and their insight that humans are linguistic beings. In the mid-1970s and onwards, Schillebeeckx came in contact with existential phenomenology. This particular school of thought insisted on the irreducibility and importance of the individual and on the discovery of the "other" in dialogue. Its influence is manifested in Schillebeeckx's use of words such as "encounter," "gift" and the "other." He was further influenced by neo-Heideggerian hermeneutics which constituted his first major shift from a Thomistic interpretive framework in terms of interpretation theory. As a result, his work on theological method and historical consciousness is influenced by neo-Heideggerian hermeneutics.

The second major shift from a Thomistic interpretive framework was the result of Schillebeeckx's contact with critical theory from the Frankfurt school of social criticism. This contact had a lasting influence on his understanding of ideologies embedded in culture, religion and language and the importance of praxis to counter evil and social injustice. Critical theory changed Schillebeeckx's theology dramatically, from his understanding of revelation to christology. The shift can also be seen in his change from an individualistic to a more social understanding of the human reality.

As a result of these changes in Schillebeeckx's interpretive framework, his theology has undergone parallel shifts in the years since 1950s. Hilkert observes three major stages in the thought of Schillebeeckx.[1] In the first stage, from the 1950s to the early 1960s, Schillebeeckx's approach to faith, revelation and experience was a "dogmatic" approach. By that Hilkert means that the starting point for Schillebeeckx's theology was the dogma of the sacrament of the Eucharist. Revelation and faith were seen primarily in terms of a sacramental existential encounter of God with humanity in history (Schillebeeckx 1967: 7-11). Revelation, in this stage of Schillebeeckx's thought, was seen as a two-step event: objective revelation and subjective revelation. Objective revelation was all contained in scripture. Subjective revelation was the interpretation of objective revelation which was new with every new interpretation, but did not introduce anything new to the core of objective revelation. Experience was seen as a witness to revelation and at no point a source of revelation, whereas faith was seen as the response to revelation.

From the mid-1960s to the 1970s, Schillebeeckx's thought underwent a shift. Hilkert calls it the historical hermeneutical shift (Hilkert 1984: 181). This shift was influenced by hermeneutical and critical theories. The starting point now was concrete human

---

1 For a detailed analysis of the development of Schillebeeckx's thought on revelation, faith and experience, see Hilkert 1984.

experience. Experience was no longer seen simply as a witness to revelation, but as the medium of revelation. Thus, there was newness in revelation. Scripture and tradition were no longer *the* sources of revelation. Rather, revelation was in the mutual critical correlation between tradition and scripture on the one hand, and contemporary situation on the other. Furthermore, praxis had become the indirect means of the verification of revelation.

According to Hilkert, there was a further fine tuning in the thought of Schillebeeckx that took place in the late 1970s and 1980s (Hilkert 1984: 185). Here, experience is not simply the medium of revelation; rather, "revelation and faith [are] dimensions of human experience" (Hilkert 1984: 185). Negative contrast experience or, in Hilkert's words, "contrast experience of human suffering becomes the central focus of Schillebeeckx's contemporary theological project" (Hilkert 1984: 186). In this stage, contrast experience takes on a major role in discerning revelation. Furthermore, praxis oriented towards liberation becomes the way in which revelation and salvation are made real, and a tool to verify the authenticity and truth claim of revelation.

My interest lies in the last two stages of Schillebeeckx's thought, where there is an intrinsic relationship between revelation and experience. In the last two stages, there is a clear concern for christology, and also Schillebeeckx is clearer on the issue of his own method. For this reason, I will restrict myself to his later works, those written between the mid-1970s and the present day.

One of the major concerns in Schillebeeckx's writings has been the contemporary question about God (Schillebeeckx 1990: 46-101). He outlines several factors that seem to have contributed to the apparent irrelevance of Christian belief in God. First, there are the external factors, such as the "collapse of social 'credibility structures' of belief in God in a secularized Western world" (1990: 46), the Cartesian dualism that characterizes such a world (1990: 47), freedom and living by choices (1990: 49), pluralism that not only changes the structure of our personality but also characterizes our cognitive reality (1990: 51), and "modernity" which acts as a "relativizing factor and therefore a challenge to belief in God" (1990: 53). The external factors also include the "world context of belief in God": our partners in dialogue differ from one place to another which, in a paradoxical way, raises the question of the universal significance of belief in God, and results in a "crisis of meaning." Second, Schillebeeckx outlines some internal factors that seem to affect belief in God. One such factor is the actual concept and image of God: "What does the word 'God' mean?" (1990: 55). Or what is the significance of "transcendence"? Another is the fact that there is a tension between belief in God and some of the church's ideology and actions: "Belief in God [is] at odds with official church morality" (1990: 61).

Thus, the question of God and our Christian system of belief seem to be irrelevant on both theoretical and practical levels. On the theoretical or intellectual level, the system of belief and the question of God seem to be unbelievable in an age characterized by historical consciousness. Schillebeeckx's work, in Jacko's words, "1) is motivated initially by the need to address the problem of pluralism in a secularized society and 2) is refined subsequently by a deepening awareness of the problems raised for theology by the particular understanding of historical contingency, relativity, temporality, and autonomy which characterizes the Western world view of the late twentieth century" (1987: 26).

On the practical level, our belief system seems even more unbelievable since a number of oppressive systems appear to use Christianity to perpetuate their control and power. Schillebeeckx gives a simple example of small-scale oppression that takes place in the name of God and Christian revelation:

> I also want to talk here about the belief in God which has expressed itself in the symbols of the patriarchal culture. Above all for women believers, belief in God has been made more difficult over the last twenty or thirty years because of the patriarchal setting in which—specifically in historical terms—the Jewish-Christian revelation of God and thus talk

> to and about God have come to us. . . . It is not so much the
> religious symbolism itself which is a stumbling block for
> many feminists, as that it also has a symbolically and
> socially oppressive effect. . . . So theological symbolism has
> in fact further intensified social and cultural discrimination
> against women. (1990: 61-62)

Thus, Schillebeeckx seeks to make sense of our belief in God in the context of our Christian faith in contemporary times. However, it is not simply a theoretical meaning that he is seeking; rather, it is an active meaning. In other words, he seeks to understand how belief in God is made actual and thus salvific in a world characterized by poverty and oppression.

Schillebeeckx gives a tentative solution to the problem. "People are the words with which God tells his story" (Schillebeeckx 1990: xiii). To speak meaningfully of God in our present-day context, we have to look at the stories of human beings, their encounters, aspirations, pains and desires, for only then can we see God and God's salvation. There is "no salvation outside the world," that is, there is no salvation in a world that is free of humans and their sufferings and aspirations, in some realm outside time or space or culture. The starting point for any meaningful talk about God is our human reality, that is, our human experience. Schillebeeckx writes: "To talk meaningfully about God is possible only on the basis of human experience" (1990: 88). "And yet for a Christian it must be clear that there is a positive link between the 'kingdom of God' and the 'kingdom of human freedom.' If here and now we nowhere experience where and how God's power is at work against evil, belief in God's omnipotence is sheer ideology, a loose statement the meaning of which cannot be verified in any way" (1990: 80). According to Schillebeeckx, meaning is intrinsically connected with the praxis of liberation, for praxis is the practical verification of the meaning of talk about and belief in God. Not only is human experience the starting point for meaningful talk about God, but praxis is the only way to maintain the integrity of our speech about God. The relationship between experience, God talk and praxis is circular: we start with experience and end with experience in the form of liberating praxis.

4.1 Historical Context: Crisis of Faith

According to Schillebeeckx, there is a "gulf between faith and experience" which "is one of the fundamental reasons for the present-day crisis among Christians who are faithful to the church" (1980b: 29).

More specifically, "the crisis lies in the fact that Jesus is still regularly explained to us as salvation and grace in terms which are no longer valid for our world of experience, i.e., in terms of *earlier* experiences; and on the other hand in the fact that we seem no longer capable in words or actions to 'make a defence for the hope that is in us' (I Peter 3.15)" (1980b: 63). The crisis that Schillebeeckx's later work seeks to address is a crisis of meaning. The crisis occurs when talk of God and salvation in Jesus, expressed in terms of a world view of another time, makes no sense and holds no meaning for us on both the intellectual and the practical levels. Schillebeeckx believes that the ground of this crisis is a split between revelation and experience. Much of the impetus for Schillebeeckx's later work is the attempt to bridge the gap between experience and revelation.

4.2 Revelatory Experience

What is revelation? For Schillebeeckx, "*revelation* is an *action* of God as *experienced* by believers and *interpreted* in religious language and therefore expressed in human terms, in the dimension of our utterly human history" (1980b: 78). Revelation is first an activity of God. It is initiated by God, and is to be characterized as a gift. However, God's address to us is not unmediated, but reaches us through the medium of experience. And precisely because it is mediated in this way, it needs to be understood. Thus, interpretation is constitutive of revelation, in that revelation, if it is to be revelation, must be understood and accepted. The acceptance of revelation implies its understanding. And because interpretation takes place within the world view, language and imagery of the time, revelation takes place in history.

Clearly, then, Schillebeeckx does not so much hold revelation and experience as two independent realities, as stress that they are intrinsically related. Experience is the medium in and through which God reveals and communicates with humans, so that "revelation has a structure of experience" (Schillebeeckx 1980b: 63). Thus, revelatory experience is a dialectical unity in a parallel manner to the dialectical unity of experience. Schillebeeckx writes: "It was said that experience is a dialectical phenomenon, an essential interweaving of encounter with the world (above all in and through actual practice), of thought and language, in a historical 'entanglement with history'. . . . Religious language shares in this dialectical interweaving of encounter with the world, thought and language. . . . In that case, religion is a particular manner of human existence, a specific form of the dialectical unity of encounter with the world, thought and language. Thus in interpretative and responsive human experiences which are put into words, revelation becomes a 'revelation' which must be formally affirmed" (1980b: 49). Revelatory experience, that is, is a dialectical unity of an encounter with reality (i.e., God), an interpretive framework (i.e., faith) and language, all taking place in history. We are now ready to analyze those different aspects of the revelatory experience that are held in tension.

4.2.1 Revelatory Experience as an Encounter with Reality — God

The first constitutive aspect of any experience is the encounter with a reality that is other than the subject. In the case of revelatory experience this reality is God. "Revelation is an action of God" (Schillebeeckx 1980b: 78). Three aspects of this need to be stressed.

The first concerns the gift-character of revelatory experience. Revelation is an action of God in that God is the initiator of the encounter, and as such is pure gift. It is grace, "a divine, salvific initiative" that manifests itself in human experiences and in history (Schillebeeckx 1979: 390). Schillebeeckx emphasizes the absolute priority of God and the divine freedom in revelation. "God cannot be reduced to a function of humanity" (Schillebeeckx 1987: 4-6). When we reduce God to our needs, God becomes a "God of the gaps." Over against this, Schillebeeckx stresses that grace is "luxury." "Thus for believers God is the luxury of their life — our luxury, not so much our cause or our final goal, but sheer, superfluous luxury" (1987: 6). Purely and simply, God is gift, a gift that is to be understood as "personal" (Schillebeeckx 1980b: 47) in that it is established within a context of relationship or, in more biblical terms, within a covenant.

The second aspect concerns the mediation of God's activity. God's activity and revelation are mediated for two intimately connected reasons. First, God is wholly other, a transcendent reality radically different from the reality of the human. God is also the creator and thus both intimate and immanent. Crucially, Schillebeeckx does not regard the transcendence and immanence of God as antithetical; rather, he argues that precisely because God is transcendent, God is immanent — the "mediated immediacy" (Schillebeeckx 1980b: 809). Schillebeeckx explains what he means by this term thus:

> What we have here is not an inter-subjective relationship between two persons — two mortal men — but a mutual relationship between a finite person and his absolute origin, the infinite God. And that has an effect on our relationship to God. In other words, we are confronted with a unique instance, an instance in which the immediacy does not do away with the mediation but in fact constitutes it. Thus from our perspective there is *mediated immediacy*. Between God and our awareness of God looms the insuperable barrier of the historical, human and natural world of creation, the constitutive symbol of the real presence of God for us. The fact that in this case an unmistakable mediation produces immediacy, instead of destroying it, is connected with the absolute or divine manner of the real presence of God: he makes him-

self directly and creatively present in the medium, that is, in
ourselves, our neighbours, the world and history. (ibid.)

Thus, God who is infinite in love and freedom communicates
with us who are finite created beings. The mediated nature of
this communication reflects the character of the relationship
between the finite order and its infinite origin in God.

The second reason for mediation is related to human reality:
"The transcending act which God is would be a thing we could
not so much as speak of—not even in faith-language—were it not
to manifest itself in the interior traffic of our world. . . . For our
speaking about God's transcendence has no ground other than
our own contingency" (Schillebeeckx 1979: 627). Or "how can we
describe the way in which reality, under the aspect in which it
does not enter our consciousness, can still be *thought* of by this
consciousness?" (Schillebeeckx 1980b: 56). Since God is totally
other than humanity, there is no way that the human person can
understand or talk about God, unless God is revealed or manifested within human reality. Thus, the question of mediation is
bound up with the question of the "hermeneutical" character of
all human knowledge. Humans cannot understand what is
beyond the created order if it is not manifested or mediated in that
created order.

Lastly—the third aspect—the God who is encountered in
the revelatory experience acts as a critical power that resists
being totally interpreted and in a way absorbed in the revelatory experience. Schillebeeckx writes: "This resistance directs all
our reflections. It reveals a reality which is independent of all
human plans, which does not come from men, but 'from elsewhere.' That does not mean that it comes from above, but rather
that something which escapes the prevailing pattern of human
knowledge makes this knowledge possible, directs it and shatters particular identifications" (1980b: 46). The resistance of
reality in revelatory experience speaks of the inability of any
revelatory experience or medium of revelation to reveal God

fully. Every revelation is also a concealment of God whose hiddenness in revelation is a critique of any possible interpretation.

All of these points add to the fact that for Schillebeeckx a revelatory experience is not, and cannot be seen as, strictly a subjective experience springing from the inner dynamics of the human subject. Initiated by God, a revelatory experience has an objective dimension, for God is always prior.

4.2.2 *Interpretive Framework as a Constitutive Aspect of Revelatory Experience*

The second constitutive aspect of any experience is the interpretive framework. Schillebeeckx means that there is no such thing as a raw experience that is only later interpreted: interpretation and experience occur simultaneously. Indeed, the interpretation is the experience; the interpretive framework is the lens through which "demonstrable elements" (Schillebeeckx 1980b: 52) are experienced. He writes: "There is no neutral given in experience, for alternative interpretations influence the very way in which we experience the world" (1980b: 53).

Revelatory experience, which again has the same structure as any other experience, also has its own interpretive frameworks, the most important of which is faith. Schillebeeckx, throughout his later work uses the expressions "revelatory experience," "experience of faith" and "religious experience" as denoting similar realities (1990: 24-33). Thus, for Schillebeeckx "we must be more specific in asserting that revelation is an interpretative experience by connecting revelation with its correlate, religious faith" (1980b: 50). Faith as an interpretive framework makes possible a different way of experiencing the world. In this connection Schillebeeckx can talk about "experience with experiences" (Schillebeeckx 1981b: 6). "People have Christian experiences in and through human experiences with men and women in our world history, within the natural environment in which we live, but always in the light of the faith-content of the Christian tradition of experience" (Schillebeeckx 1990: 25). Thus, faith does not simply offer a different interpretation of the so-called "demonstrable elements" in the world, such as evil or order, but rather the world with its evil and order is experienced differently. For a non-believer these elements may simply aggravate the feelings of contingency and finitude, while for believers they may be the means in and through which they experience the loving-kindness of God, where God's infinity grounds and carries their finitude. Thus, "not only does the religious man interpret in a different way from the non-believer, he lives in a different world and has different experiences. Thus for the believer the exodus through the Red Sea can in fact be taken as an expression of an *experience* and not as a secondary interpretation or a superstructure which can be detached from this context of experience" (Schillebeeckx 1980b: 50).

Faith as an interpretive framework in revelatory experience is both a stance or an attitude and content. Both are interrelated and form the horizon through which human experiences are experienced as revelatory. Furthermore, the content of faith as "a reflective expression of a collective experience of a group of religious people" (Schillebeeckx 1990: 24) can be seen as that which forms tradition. In this sense, tradition is another interpretive framework constitutive of revelatory experience: thus, tradition cannot be pitted against experience, since tradition is constitutive of religious experience. World view, philosophy and cultural forms in conjunction with faith and tradition further shape the interpretive framework that is constitutive of a revelatory experience.[2]

Finally, there is a certain "newness" to revelation. The title of Schillebeeckx's book *God Is New Each Moment* (1983), reflects clearly his belief in the possibility of "the new" in God's revelation. He writes: "With regard to what has already been achieved, [God] is always absolutely new. He is never exhausted, certainly

---

2 Louis Dupré (1982) disagrees with Schillebeeckx on the issue of the interpretive frameworks in experience, especially revelatory experience. Dupré claims that it is impossible to separate experience from its interpretive frameworks or models. Those interpretive frameworks have to be as authoritative as the revelatory experience itself. By contrast, Schillebeeckx thinks that interpretive frameworks, although constitutive of the revelatory experience, are historically conditioned and therefore change from age to age.

never in the kingdom that he establishes among us. There is always openness. We have to leave God his freedom in being new with regard to us. . . . I prefer to see God not as an unchangeable and unchanging God, but rather as eternal youth. . . . God is new each day. He is a constant source of new possibilities. This is true not only with regard to our history, but also with regard to the end of our history — the eschaton. He is always surprising us" (1983: 29). The newness is manifested in new interpretations of our lives and our identity. It is also manifested in conversion which leads to lifestyle changes. This newness is "experienced" as a gratuitous gift from God (Schillebeeckx 1990: 22). In this light, namely, the newness of revelation, Schillebeeckx understands the event of Jesus Christ. The stories in the New Testament are testimonies to new experiences of grace that open up new ways of life in which all are invited to participate. In Schillebeeckx's words, "The narrative character of testimonies to new experiences through which a new way of life is also opened to others is a mark of the whole of the New Testament. In all its writings it is the story of new experiences — of experiences of grace" (1980b: 42). Precisely because revelation is relational, the source of the newness in experiences of grace is both God and the human person. Of course, God's unconditional love and concern for the human does not change, for God is faithful. But God is the source of the newness precisely because God is the source of the "experience" of grace. On the other hand, one can also say that an element of newness resides in the interpretive ability of the human; the possibility of "the new" derives from the possibility of new interpretations. Moreover, since new interpretations result from modified interpretive frameworks which change along with history and culture, there will always be new interpretations and thus new "experiences" of grace.[3]

---

3 Language is the third component in the dialectical unity that forms experience. However, what is said about language in revelatory experience is the same as that about language in experience. Thus, I will defer discussion of this to a later part of this chapter.

4.2.3 Revelatory Experience As Articulated in History

Schillebeeckx identifies two major implications of historicity for an understanding of revelation: first, the limitedness and the historical and cultural conditioning of all revelatory experiences; and second, the fact that no priority can be accorded to one particular age or time, especially the past, in assessing revelation. All of history is important: the present and the future, not only the past; history as a whole is the locus of revelation.

First of all, historical consciousness raises the questions of the contingency and plurality of revelatory experiences – as Schillebeeckx puts it, "the reality which occurs as history reveals itself both as a potential unity and as a plurality of events that cannot be eliminated" (1979: 615). In other words, we can talk about and even experience the absolute but we cannot do so absolutely. Although God reveals the divine self through the created order, this order, composed of human experiences and history, cannot capture God. God remains the totally transcendent God. Thus, Schillebeeckx can say that "God makes himself known in and through human experiences as the one who transcends all closely described experiences" (1987: 42). God is always greater than any medium, even if we claim that in and through that medium the definitive revelation of God is disclosed. This applies even to Jesus. "God is greater than even his supreme, decisive and definitive revelation of himself in the man Jesus" (Schillebeeckx 1987: 16-17).

Furthermore, our experience of revelation is conditioned and mediated through culture, society and history (Schillebeeckx 1984b: 42). This means, therefore, that the revelatory experience is not simply private, without reference to the subject's cultural and historical situation. Schillebeeckx writes: "Every experience of a human person, granted all its originality, stands at the same time in a tradition of social experience and is never a simple drawing upon some interior plenitude without any mediatory factors" (1979: 658). Once again, although God's revelation can be perceived in and through human experience, it does not simply emerge from human experience. In other words, "the self-revelation of God does not manifest itself from our experiences but in them; . . . thus human beings are in no way the ground of revelation" (Schillebeeckx 1981b: 12-13). Revelation is therefore understood as a transcendent reality that is manifested in the horizon of our history (1980d: 48).

The second point that is raised by historical consciousness is the fact that the past, exemplified in the life of the early church or the Greek fathers, is no more privileged than our own time as the locus of revelatory experience. All of history is the medium of God's revelation. However, this statement is not to be understood in terms of God acting above or alongside human history (Schillebeeckx 1990: 221). Scripture is a privileged medium insofar as it is the record of the original experiences of the encounter with Jesus Christ. However, scripture is not the only locus of revelation.

For contemporary humanity the locus of God's revelation is the present time. Schillebeeckx emphasizes the importance of secular history, for through the mediation of human beings secular history becomes salvation history (1987: 31). That is the reason why Schillebeeckx takes the phenomenon of secularization seriously. Furthermore, he does not hesitate to borrow or make use of what his modern culture can offer, for that is where God speaks. Revelation and "experiences" are not opposed to each other. On the contrary, God's revelation follows the course of human experiences as articulated in history (Schillebeeckx 1981b: 11).

4.2.4 What Is Revealed?

It is important at this juncture to discuss the content of the revelatory experience. Since revelatory experience is an encounter between God and humanity mediated in and through the world in history, it follows that this encounter must reveal something about both God and humanity. Revelatory experience reveals that God is faithful and that the presence of God is continuous in our midst. It reveals God's salvation as concern for humanity, and that this salvation is experienced as promise: an eschatolog-

ical proviso that includes a critical dimension (Schillebeeckx
1980b: 777). In other words, salvation can become actual only in
the free and active role of humans in liberating praxis towards
one another. God's salvation is both gift and task.

If we maintain that revelation is relational, then it also has to
reveal something about human reality. God is revealed as direct-
ing saving activity towards humanity. The content of revelation
is that "man's cause [is] God's cause" (Schillebeeckx 1979: 229),
and that God's concern is for humanity. Human happiness is a
matter of pride to God, and the salvation of the human person is
seen as glorification of the grace of God (Schillebeeckx 1980b:
512). This is how Schillebeeckx understands the kingdom of
God. The "definition of God's rule [is] having man as its central
concern" (Schillebeeckx 1979: 652). Schillebeeckx even understands sin as that act or attitude that hurts God insofar as it is
harmful to God's creatures (1987: 31). Thus, what constitutes
revelation of the divine self is the salvation of humanity.

Here, we reach a crucial point in Schillebeeckx's theology.
Schillebeeckx does not deny that experiences of meaning reveal
God. However, it is experiences of meaninglessness that reveal
the critical power of God's presence and reveal God's salvation.
Experiences of evil and oppression evoke a critical response. Any
project that does not have human concern at its centre is critiqued
and rejected by God in and through the life and message of Jesus
Christ. "All other orientations and projects that do not start from
the priority of God's future for man are criticized by Jesus"
(Schillebeeckx 1979: 140). One must understand God's presence
as one that exerts a critical function (Schillebeeckx 1975b: 7).

The life and message of Jesus reveal that God, who is concerned with human happiness, rejects oppression. Moreover,
God rejects the human self-understanding that allows oppression to continue.

This critical function of God's revelation further prompts
humanity into action in order to resist any denigration and
oppression of the human. Thus, revelation leads the human into

the proper praxis to resist evil. The process of any attempt at liberation in history is the medium of God's revelation. "Only in a secular history in which men and women are liberated for true humanity can God reveal his own being. There are also many histories of suffering and disaster in secular history; God cannot reveal himself in them except . . . as a veto or as judgment" (Schillebeeckx 1990: 7). In other words, salvation is brought about through humans freeing and liberating each other (1990: 162). What is revealed in revelation is the divine self. But the revelation of God's faithfulness and love is manifested as concern for humanity and human happiness. This revelation is not only mediated in and through human praxis for liberation; it also prompts liberation.

4.3 The Doctrine of Creation

According to Schillebeeckx, "the concept of creation is of fundamental significance in any theology of grace. If man is left alone with a world for man which is not at the same time and more fundamentally the world of God, the assurance of faith remains in the subjectivity of man and is therefore constantly exposed to the suspicion of being a pure projection. The God of the universe, and also of nature, is one of the elements which can keep open the religious subjectivity of 'subjectivism'" (1980b: 530). The importance given to experience in mediating God's self-revelation is grounded in an understanding of revelation and God's activity. Furthermore, Schillebeeckx believes that God's salvation is mediated in the human praxis of liberation. The ground of both beliefs (that is, belief in the mediation of God's revelation and belief in God's salvation in the created order, especially in human experience and liberating praxis) is in Schillebeeckx's positive outlook and his understanding of the doctrine of creation.[4]

For Schillebeeckx, the doctrine of creation highlights several points that are important for his theology. First, creation is the

---

4 For a detailed analysis of Schillebeeckx's understanding of creation, see Jacko 1987: 85-129.

symbol of "God's loving perseverance with the finite — the lowly" (Schillebeeckx 1981b: 112). The doctrine of creation affirms that what God created was and is good. Hence, Schillebeeckx wants to emphasize that the contingency and finitude of creation are not things that must be overcome nor are they a result of sin. Rather, finitude is simply creation's otherness from God, which God deemed to be good. According to Schillebeeckx, "Jewish-Christian belief in creation . . . says that God is God, the sun is the sun . . . and man is man, and moreover that God's blessing rests precisely upon that: this is how it is good. It is good that man is simply man . . . i.e., not-God, contingent: they could just as well not have been, yet they are thought to be worth the difficulty and the price" (1981b: 113). Furthermore, it is through the finitude of creation that God is able to reveal the divine self. Thus, "nature and history are authorities in and through which God reveals himself as creator in and through our fundamental experiences of finitude" (1981b: 116). The created order is good, and God abides in and reveals God's self in and through its finitude.

Second, to believe that creation is both contingent and good is also to hold that creation is unfinished. Creation is ever-growing; sins are the result not of "fallen" nature but of the growing pains of adulthood. Thus, the core of creation-centred theology is not sin, but rather the positivity of creation. It follows that, because of the incomplete nature of the created world, the human person as a co-creator with God has a responsibility to finish God's work. In this way, the human person is able to do God's work and to be the free instrument of God's salvation. In Schillebeeckx's words, "God creates human beings as the principle of their own human lives, so that human action has to develop and effectuate the world and its future in human solidarity, within contingent situations and given boundaries, and therefore with respect for both inanimate and animate nature. . . . [God] creates human beings with a free human will, freely to develop their own human future, to realize it in contingent, chance and also specific situations" (1990: 230-31).

More specifically, God's salvation is made real and actual in and through human actions of liberation. Thus, it is human praxis that completes God's creative work in creation, and the coming Kingdom of God is mediated by humans who care for each other (Schillebeeckx 1979: 153).

Third, the proof of the positivity of creation is in Jesus Christ. Jesus is understood as the proof that God's trust in humanity has not been put to shame, since Christians believe that God's salvation has come to the world through the life, ministry and death of the human Jesus of Nazareth. In Schillebeeckx's words, "In Jesus, both God's trust in man and man's response of trust in God take on their definitive historical form. Jesus is alpha and omega." (1981b: 109).

Finally, belief in the creator God and the goodness of creation exerts a critical power. It critiques unrealistic visions of humanity and human history, whether they are too optimistic or too pessimistic (Schillebeeckx 1981b: 118). Schillebeeckx calls this critical force the "proviso of the creator God." This proviso "means that the possible despair which the finitude of our existence can produce in us is taken up by God's absolute presence in his finite world of creation; and this presence is a stimulus towards constantly renewed hope" (1981b: 119). However, that is not all. The proviso of the creator God not only renews hope in the face of despair and evil; it also acts as an impetus to change and to counter evil. It acts as an imperative for action: liberating action. "God is essentially a champion of the good and an opponent of all evil, injustice and suffering. . . . Seen in this light, for the believer the inspiration and orientation of all action can be found only in a call to further all good and justice and to oppose all evil, injustice and suffering in all its forms" (1981b: 120).

In summary, the belief in creation grounds Schillebeeckx's understanding of the importance of the human as co-creator with God, in whose actions God mediates salvation. Thus, God's revelation and salvation are mediated in human experience and action, while at the same time revelation critiques those actions.

5

A HERMENEUTICAL THEORY

Another aspect of the question of historical consciousness with which Schillebeeckx has been preoccupied is that of change and pluralism. In this chapter, I will present Schillebeeckx's theory of history and historical change, and then proceed to his understanding of hermeneutics.

5.1 An Understanding of History

Schillebeeckx's reflection on historical change focuses on identifying that which forms the continuous thread in the midst of the change, the unchanging within the change. He proposes that, "within the one historical process there are discernible at least three planes, which are not however adjacent or parallel but enfold and interpenetrate one another, and together constitute the one history of human kind" (1979: 577). Elsewhere, the image Schillebeeckx uses is that of concentric circles moving around an axis (1989b: 307-19). The circle closest to the axis moves the slowest; and as the circle's distance from the axis increases, the rotation of that circle also increases. Thus, the circle furthest from the centre is the fastest moving.

The first circle or plane of history "is 'fact-constituted history' or 'ephemeral history,' with its brief and rapidly expiring rhythm: the events of every day come and go" (Schillebeeckx 1979: 577). In this first plane, or the first or largest concentric circle as it were, the change is rapid and does not have a lasting effect. The second plane of history is "'conjunctural history,' which is more expansive, has a more profound reach and is more comprehensive, but then at a much slower tempo or rate of change; in other words, a cultural conjuncture lasts for a long time" (ibid.). Finally, there is the third plane of history, the last concentric circle, which is the closest to the axis as it were. Schillebeeckx writes: "Lastly, there is 'structural history,' with a time-span of centuries, almost bordering on the central point between what moves and what does not, although not standing outside history. . . . Actually, in the third plane the process of change is extremely cumbersome and slow; basic structures survive even the most radical of revolutions" (ibid.). Thus, the various sectors in history do not move at the same rate: there are the very fast-moving aspects that do not seem to have lasting influences; there are slower-moving aspects that span lifetimes; and finally there are those aspects that span centuries and seem to be almost unchanging.

However, "what is true of culture as a whole applies also to sub-sectors and cultural vectors, as also to 'human thinking' (and so to thinking motivated by religious belief)" (Schillebeeckx 1979: 577). In human thinking there are three planes which are intrinsically related and do not move at the same rate, i.e., they move non-synchronously. "In man's evolving intellective life (and religious life) there are circling round an all but stationary depth-element which we have called structural the somewhat faster-moving circle of conjuncturally conditioned thinking and, on the outermost rim of these concentric circles, the fleeting thoughts of every passing day, with their often 'modish' aspects" (ibid.). Schillebeeckx is particularly interested in the inner and middle circles, and their relationship to what he calls the "epochal horizon of the intellect" (ibid.) or interpretive frameworks. For these interpretative frameworks are the horizon through which a particular experience is what it is. He writes: "Now what has been called the 'epochal horizon of the intellect,' or thinking done within the bounds of 'interpretative models' (with the mark of a particular period upon them) or a horizon of 'current' experience — all this I would put in the second plane of 'history'; in other words, the particular horizon of experience and intellection, conditioned by the spirit of the age, belongs to 'conjunctural history' . . . a given intellective horizon, therefore, persists through a whole period" (1979: 577-78). If the "conjunctural" plane in human thought is composed of an interpretive framework formed by the philosophy of the time, world view and such, does it follow that the innermost circle, that is the "structural history," is constituted by unchanging ideas and concepts? Here, Schillebeeckx is clear that "we do not mean to say that in addition to changing concepts in man's thinking there are also lastingly valid concepts which can be supposed to survive intact every more or less fundamental shift in the experiential or world horizon" (1979: 578). By contrast, "we do mean that the basic structure of human thinking asserts itself in the conjuncturally conditioned ideas and in the changing horizon of man's understanding and experience" (ibid.). Thus, it is precisely because of this same basic human structure of thinking, which changes very slowly, that we are able to understand a different "conjunctural" interpretive horizon of thinking. However, this tension between the "structural" and the "conjunctural" horizons of thinking not only makes possible the understanding of other times; but also is the cause of irritation and alienation. In Schillebeeckx's words, "the reason for this is the dialectical tension between the conjunctural and structural aspects of the thinking; it is this tension in particular that makes each history ambivalent — a constant imperative to engage in interpretation, which itself stands within the ambiguity of history" (ibid.). This dialectical tension results in ambiguity and thus the "imperative to engage in interpretation." It is the ground of hermeneutics.

Finally, how is it that we, who live in a particular conjunctural plane of history and who cannot live outside it, are able to recognize other conjunctural planes of history? Schillebeeckx's answer is: "This history with its ambiguity is surmounted, but not annulled, by our 'time-consciousness,' by means of which we do in some measure transcend the 'lived' temporality, not, it is true, in a *conscience survolante* but still in an 'openness' to the Mystery which encompasses all 'history'" (1979: 578-79).

In summary, Schillebeeckx's understanding of history makes interpretation an imperative. World views and philosophies that fall within the conjunctural plane change with time. However, that which is continuous or unchanging is the structural elements. Thus, an important element in interpretation, especially interpretation of scripture, is the ability to identify those structural elements that are unchanging and those world views and philosophies that fall within the conjunctural plane. Only then can we come to a faithful interpretation of our faith. Interpretation here is not limited to the interpretation of texts, but includes the interpretation of reality, including the reality that is behind the texts.

5.2 A Hermeneutics of History[1]

For Schillebeeckx, the attempt to find faithful interpretations of Scripture and faith raises at a fundamental level the question of human historicity. God's word, given in and through the historically conditioned human word, is not immune from human historicity, for "God's word is given to us within the already interpretative response to it of the Old and the New Testaments. . . . The God of salvation was made the subject of a conversation between men — it was in this way that God's word was addressed to us" (Schillebeeckx 1977: 5).

Although expressed here in one of Schillebeeckx's earlier writings, this nevertheless forms the consistent basis of his understanding of hermeneutics. He proposes a "hermeneutics of history": "I shall both formulate the problem as clearly as possible and analyse and criticize the new solutions, in order to open up, via hermeneutics of history, a perspective within which, in my opinion, faithfulness to the biblical message in interpretation of faith will continue to be guaranteed" (1977: 4-5). Schillebeeckx out-

---

1 For a detailed analysis of Schillebeeckx's "hermeneutics of history," see Hilkert 1984: 103-35.

lines three aspects of this "hermeneutics of history" in an attempt to deal adequately with the problem of faithful interpretation.

First, the past is always renewed in the light of the present. Schillebeeckx believes that the distance that separates us from the past is not a hindrance or an obstacle that must be overcome for us to arrive at an objective interpretation of the past. On the contrary, "the distance in time, which was often characterized in the past as an obstacle to objective interpretation of texts and of history that had to be overcome, is now seen rather as the ontological condition that makes this interpretation possible" (Schillebeeckx 1977: 24-25). A corollary of this is that no one can stand in a neutral place from which objective interpretations can be undertaken; each person must stand in his or her own tradition. "Understanding outside a tradition is humanly inconceivable, since such an understanding involves a fundamental misconception of the ontological pre-structure and of the condition that makes all human understanding possible. On the basis of our essential being as men understanding is a reinterpretative understanding of tradition—an understanding of tradition in the manner of reinterpretation" (Schillebeeckx 1977: 27). Furthermore, Schillebeeckx is not so much interested in texts of scripture in and for themselves as in the reality to which they refer[2]. Thus, "taking the texts themselves as his point of departure, the interpreter therefore goes beyond the texts and their meaning and inquires about the reality to which the texts intentionally or unintentionally bear witness" (Schillebeeckx 1977: 33).

Second, both the present and the past are within the sphere of the promise. This second aspect of the "hermeneutics of history" is a way of speaking of the Pauline "already and not yet." For Schillebeeckx, to look at only the present and the past is to fall into the trap of existential theologians such as Bultmann (Schillebeeckx 1977: 35). Thus, "every interpretation of the past in the light of the present is, after all, open to the future and ori-

---

2 In a sense, Schillebeeckx's seeking of the "reality" to which the text is a witness is a direct critique of the view that supports the "linguisticality of reality." In this, Schillebeeckx is a realist, who holds to an objective reality outside language, albeit experienced within language.

ented towards it. The future is not, of course, to be interpreted, but it certainly has to be realized and, what is more, it should bring something new into being" (1977: 35-36). The last clause is very important, highlighting the fact that for Schillebeeckx the "eschatological proviso" or the understanding that our faith stands under God's promise, which must become actual in and through our own work, becomes an impetus for action. In other words, "there certainly is a 'deposit of faith,' but its content still remains, on the basis of the promise already realized in Christ, a promise-for-us, with the result that interpretation becomes 'hermeneutics of praxis'. . . . But it is not interpretation which has the last word, but orthopraxis, making everything new by virtue of God's promise" (1977: 37-38).

Third, there is a certain permanence in the present, past and future. On this point Schillebeeckx is critical of Bultmann, Gadamer, Pannenberg and Moltmann. He writes: "These thinkers [post-Bultmann, Gadamer, Pannenberg and Moltmann] have lost sight of another decisive aspect of man's temporality — that is, of the fact that our historicity involves not only lived temporality but also consciousness of time. This consciousness of time, which can also, of its nature, be conceptualized, implies a certain transcendence of temporality" (1977: 38). We have already touched on this point in discussing humans' ability to recognize the different planes of history (the "conjunctural" and the "structural") although they cannot be outside history. Schillebeeckx here refers to the human ability to transcend time by being able both to stand back and critique past actions and to project into the future while remaining rooted in the present — in other words, to be conscious of time.

Thus, transcendence of temporality can be seen as an openness. The question is, openness to what? According to Schillebeeckx, the transcendence of temporality is an openness to mystery. According to him, "it [transcendence of temporality] does imply a real openness in our temporality, something which could almost be called a 'trans-historical' element" (1977: 39).

Thus, what constitutes permanence in the present, the past and the future is, on the one hand, human openness and, on the other, the presence of mystery. Permanence is not constituted by unchanging dogma.

From here we turn to the relationship between experience and hermeneutics. Is there a relationship between how we understand or interpret the world and the way in which we experience or encounter the world? Schillebeeckx's answer is affirmative. Interpretation and experience relate to each other; indeed, interpretation is constitutive of experience, so that there is no experience that is not already interpreted.

5.3 An Analysis of Experience

Schillebeeckx defines experience thus: "Experience is a dialectical phenomenon, an essential interweaving of encounter with the world (above all in and through actual practice), of thought and language, in a historical 'entanglement with history.' Human existence *is* this dialectical interweaving" (1980b: 49). Experience is a dialectical unity within human life of four different realities, each one of which is constitutive of experience: an encounter with reality or the world; thought, or what has been referred to earlier as "interpretive frameworks"; language; and, finally, history.[3]

5.3.1 Encounter with Reality or the World

Interpreted experience is not subjective but is an encounter with a reality that is outside the subject — a reality that is other, the world. In Schillebeeckx's words, "It emerges from this that man is a constructive, rational being: a *projecting* existence. Nevertheless, reality remains the final criterion: it can destroy all our projects or at least weigh them down or change them" (1980b: 34). Thus, the reality that the subject encounters in the experience exerts a criti-

---

3 Gelpi (1994) critiques Schillebeeckx's construct of experience because in the final analysis, in Gelpi's opinion, Schillebeeckx's construct will not be able to give account of the divinity of Jesus.

cal power, which can force a change in models and interpretive frameworks. The interpretive frameworks that form the horizon of our experiences change from one age to another due to the dynamic relationship between what Schillebeeckx calls thinking and perceiving (1980b: 31). An important aspect of this dynamic relationship is what Schillebeeckx calls "the resistance of reality."

> Men live by guesses and hypotheses, projects and constructs, and therefore by trial and error; their projects can constantly be blocked by the resistance or the refractoriness of reality, which will not always fit in with these rational anticipations. . . . But where reality offers resistance to such outlines and implicitly therefore guides them in an indirect way, we come into contact with a reality which is *independent* of us, which is not thought of, made or projected by men. At this point, we have a revelation of that which cannot be manipulated, a "transcendent" power, something that comes "from elsewhere," which asserts its validity in the face of our projects and nevertheless makes all human plans, products and considerations possible, by virtue of its critical and negative orientation. . . . Surprising, unexpected, new ways of perceiving are opened up in and through the resistance presented by reality. (1980b: 34-35)

The resistance of some elements of our experiences, that is, our inability to fit these elements into already existing models and paradigms, forces us to change these paradigms and models. Thus, that which does not make perceiving and thinking coincident is the so-called "resistance of reality"; and interpretive frameworks change in an attempt to accommodate this "resistance of reality."

5.3.2 Interpretive Frameworks or Thought

The function of interpretive frameworks in constituting experience is underlined by Schillebeeckx when he uses the terms "interpreted experience" (1980b: 33) and the interweaving of "perception and thought" (1980b: 31).

In stressing that all experience is interpreted experience, Schillebeeckx refers to the fact that interpretation is not simply an intellectual exercise set in motion after a particular raw experience has been lived, for there is no such thing as a raw or neutral experience that is understood or interpreted in a subsequent step. Over against this kind of Cartesian dualism of subject and object, Schillebeeckx insists that "we experience in the act of interpreting, without being able to draw a neat distinction between the element of experience and the element of interpretation" (1980b: 33). The particular and concrete way in which one experiences reality is, at the same time, the particular and concrete way in which one understands and interprets that reality. Thus, the relationship between interpretation and experience is not an extrinsic relationship, where one can exist without the other. On the contrary, interpretation is intrinsic to experience; or, in other words, interpretation is constitutive of experience. "Interpretation does not begin only when questions are asked about the significance of what one has experienced. Interpretative identification is already an intrinsic element of the experience itself, first unexpressed and then deliberately reflected on" (Schillebeeckx 1981b: 13). However, as mentioned in the section on "hermeneutics of history," interpretation and understanding are also constituted by praxis, and thus the "hermeneutics of praxis." Interpretation is not simply an intellectual exercise, but an actualization of a way of understanding. Another way of describing this relationship between experience and interpretation is to use the concept of perceiving and thinking. "Experience is gained in a dialectical fashion: through an interplay between perception and thought, thought and perception . . . the connection between experience and thought is rather that the constantly unforeseen content of new experiences keeps forcing us to think again" (Schillebeeckc 1980b: 31-32).

Although interpretation and experience are intrinsically related to each other, one can separate them for the sake of analysis, and talk of interpretive frameworks or, in simpler terms, models. Schillebeeckx writes: "The recognition has grown that the theory or the model has a certain primacy over the experience; at any rate, in the sense that on the one hand there can be no experiences without at least an implicit theory, and on the other, that theories cannot be derived from experiences by induction, but are the result of the creative initiative of the human spirit" (1981b: 17). Interpretive frameworks thus are understood as the horizons in and through which experiences are interpreted. They are constituted by time-bound philosophies and world views, images and concepts, models and paradigms; such is their role in experience that Schillebeeckx can claim that "there is no experience without 'theorizing'; without guesses, hypotheses and theories. . . . We experience reality — on all these levels — always through models of reality" (1980b: 34).

5.3.3 *Language*

Language is also constitutive of experience, because the interpretive frameworks are in language. Schillebeeckx discusses the issue of language in the context of revelatory experience: "The very fact that revelation comes to us in human language — as in the Old and New Testament — shows that revelation is essentially concerned with human experience. However, language is the deposit of a common *experience*. Revelation is experience expressed in the word; it is God's saving action as experienced and communicated *by men*" (1980b: 46).

Schillebeeckx, however, is critical of the principle that meaning is use, and of those who hold to the "linguisticality of reality," i.e., that language is constitutive of reality. According to Schillebeeckx, "the crisis in the churches points clearly enough to the inadequacy of the principle of 'language-meaning from use' which is employed by certain linguistic analysts and which can be briefly defined as the principle that the meaning of language is determined by the language game in which it is used" (1975b: 14). The crisis is that this language game is no longer understood by believers themselves. It has become meaningless for the fol-

pretive frameworks; in this sense, it forces a change in these ideas. Furthermore, the "negative contrast experience" of suffering and oppression forces a change by disclosing the destructive tendencies in our ideas and world view; these experiences also force a change, not only in the ideas themselves, but also in their application. Thus, "the human experience of suffering and evil, of oppression and unhappiness, is the basis and source of a fundamental 'no' that men and women say to their actual situation of being-in-this-world" (Schillebeeckx 1990: 5).

5.4 Criteria for Christian Interpretation

What are the criteria for a faithful interpretation of the Christian message? What are the criteria for the meaning and truth of statements about God? Although Schillebeeckx's answers to these questions are set forth primarily in his earlier work, his later work is consistent with his earlier thinking.[4]

Schillebeeckx divides the question of theological hermeneutics into two parts: "First, how can a Christian who believes in the Biblical message of the kingdom of God understand this message in the twentieth century and how can he justify this new, contemporary interpretation as a Christian interpretation? Secondly, how can he, within the many different religious and non-religious interpretations of the world and of human life which surround him, justify his Christian interpretation of reality with regard to modern thought or at least when faced with the legitimate demands of modern thinking?" (1975b: ix). Schillebeeckx concentrates mainly on the first part of the hermeneutical question. That is, his concern is with the faithful or orthodox reinterpretation of the Christian message in our contemporary experience.

It has been made clear that Schillebeeckx's project was hermeneutical from the start, concerning problems of meaning.

---

4 Schillebeeckx's later work is consistent with his earlier work on the issue of adequate criteria of interpretation. The linguistic criteria of meaning are implicit in his book *The Understanding of Faith*, especially pp. 16-19. The theological criteria for truth, such as praxis and the proportionate norm, are more explicit in *Church: The Human Story of God*, pp. 5-8, 41-42.

However, the question of truth has never been far from his mind. Indeed, the way in which he understands truth informs his understanding of the meaning of the Christian message. For Schillebeeckx, "the question of meaning is connected with that of truth, but they are not identical. From the point of view of phenomenology and linguistic analysis, the question of meaning precedes the question of truth: only a meaningful statement can be true or false and a meaningless affirmation is neither true nor false" (1975b: 86). Meaning reflects Schillebeeckx's concern with the relevance of the Christian message, while truth is concerned with the faithful interpretation of that message. The priority of meaning over truth is reflected in the crisis of which Schillebeeckx speaks. The crisis of faith is primarily a crisis of meaning and secondarily one of truth.

5.4.1 Criteria for Meaning: Linguistic Criteria

Precisely because of the centrality of the biblical text for Christianity, linguistic criteria for meaning become paramount. Schillebeeckx writes: "From the very beginning of Christianity the problem of theological hermeneutics has been connected essentially with the bible" (1975b: 20). However, Schillebeeckx warns that, although interpreting the Bible is essential for the understanding of Christianity, it is the reality to which the text witnesses that is the goal of interpretation, and not simply the text. Thus, "in both cases [interpreting the Old and New Testaments] as in every case of literary interpretation, it is not simply a question of interpreting a text. Interpreting the Old Testament is interpreting a reality and a history in the light of faith in Yahweh. . . . What we have is a reality to be interpreted, but this is done via a literature that itself has to be interpreted" (ibid.).

There are three different schools of linguistic philosophy from which Schillebeeckx draws his insights. However, Schillebeeckx does not necessarily accept all their presuppositions.

5.4.1.1 Structural Linguistic Analysis

Schillebeeckx defines structural linguistic analysis as "a study of language simply as an institution, that is, as a structure independent of the subject who is speaking, and of which the individual may even be unconscious" (1975b: 23). In other words, structural analysis puts the speaking subject on hold, seeing language as a closed system of signs whose meaning resides in the relationship between a particular sign and other signs in that system. It is a way of arriving at "objective meaning" independent of the subject. Thus, "language is therefore above all a system of relationships in which a word or a term has no meaning of its own apart from being a sign which is distinguished, within the linguistic system, from all other linguistic signs" (Schillebeeckx 1975b: 23-24). The insight from structural analysis that Schillebeeckx regards as important for theological hermeneutics is this: "Structuralism emphasizes the possibility that these words may have different meanings, but at the same time, insists that not all of these various meanings have to be present in every context, or in fact are present. If this is overlooked, words tend to be isolated from their syntax, with the consequence that contextual meanings are made independent and raised to the level of universal concepts and used to support a theology of the old or new testaments" (1975b: 25). Structuralism "can help us to expose many prejudices and even more important, many unjustified generalizations in theological hermeneutics" (1975b: 26).

5.4.1.2 Phenomenological Linguistic Analysis

Phenomenological analysis of language, for Schillebeeckx, like structuralism, starts with a reduction of language: it puts reality on hold. "In this case, judgment about reality is suspended and that reality is, as it were, placed in brackets. In itself, this reduction has no metaphysical claims. All that is involved is the structure of the phenomenon as such" (Schillebeeckx 1975b: 26-27). According to Schillebeeckx, phenomenological linguistic analysis seeks to understand the "relationship of language as a system of signs and the verbal event as an intentionality" (1975b: 27). Language "is therefore not thought of in isolation, but is seen in its mediating function as an offer of meaning (its referential and representative aspect), as self-expression and as communication" (ibid.). The intentionality of speech refers to the fact that the speaker says something, which constitutes "meaning," about an object, which constitutes "reference" to someone (ibid.). Thus, the structure of the verbal event is triadic, involving the speaker, the listeners and the subject matter, and language is therefore seen as an instrument of self-expression, meaning and communication (1975b: 29). Language expresses the being-in-the-world of the speaker, communicating "the referential and representational aspect of language as conveying meaning" (1975b: 28). Schillebeeckx summarizes the importance of phenomenology for theological hermeneutics under three headings. "In the first place, there is the need for a critically analysed pre-understanding in any interpretation of the Bible" (1975b: 31). Schillebeeckx acknowledges the fact that we come to the biblical text with preconceived ideas. However, for the biblical text to be understood adequately, our preconceived ideas have to be critically analyzed through examination of our situation and agendas. "In the second place, the movement of this process of interpretation is circular. Our point of departure is a definite pre-understanding, but our intention is to gain a new understanding" (ibid.). Here, Schillebeeckx is drawing attention to the hermeneutical circle, where we start with a pre-understanding that becomes modified, changed or discarded upon our reading ofthe Bible. The meaning of the Bible transforms our pre-understanding into understanding, which then becomes the pre-understanding of a new reading of the Bible. "In the third place, theological re-interpretation is only possible if the interpreter has other ways of speaking at his disposal" (ibid.). In a sense, this is similar to the situation where a person attempts to translate an English verse: it is impossible if the translator does not know any other language. In similar fashion, one cannot translate a myth into another myth. However, a myth can be translated into philosophical or theological language. Finally, Schillebeeckx draws attention to the fact that, in theological interpretation, the self-expression aspect of the triadic structure of communication is more pronounced. "The existential aspect which characterizes all verbal expressions, the aspect of self-expression, is much deeper in the case of a religious language situation, since what is expressed in such a situation is total existence. . . . Theological interpretation of the Bible is therefore also an existential interpretation of the Bible" (1975b: 32).

5.4.1.3 Logical Linguistic Analysis

The third school of thought upon which Schillebeeckx draws is logical linguistic analysis. Its concern is the issue of meaning. For "the first question that is asked by logical analysis is always the critical question of meaning, and this question is asked in such a way as to establish no valid limit a priori to the possible meaning of any proposition" (Schillebeeckx 1975b: 33). Prior to the question of truth is the question of meaningfulness. Only if a statement is meaningful can the subsequent question of its truth be asked. "Logical analysis, then, insists on the fundamental distinction between 'untruth' and 'meaningless.' Propositions can be meaningful or meaningless, but only meaningful propositions can be true or untrue" (1975b: 34). Thus, logical linguistic analysis also reduces language: whereas structuralism puts the subject on hold, and phenomenological analysis puts reality on hold, logical linguistic analysis puts the issue of truth on hold. Schillebeeckx states: "The point of departure for logical linguistic analysis [is] a reduction which by-passes the content and confines itself to logical, formal and structural rules" (1975b: 35).

But what of the contribution of logical linguistic analysis to theological hermeneutics? Its contribution is that it enables philosophers and theologians alike to set aside questions that are in reality a result of the misuse of language, questions that originate in category mistakes and thus are not real questions. In

Schillebeeckx's words, "this is the unmistakable, although of course obvious contribution made by logical analysis, enabling many philosophical or theological problems to be set aside at the very outset as pseudo-problems" (1975b: 34).

This kind of linguistic analysis compels theologians to be coherent. "Even the theologian cannot, within one and the same point of view in time and space, at the same time affirm and deny something" (Schillebeeckx 1975b: 35). And not only does it force theologians to be internally consistent by recognizing the different language games and their limits, but it also raises the question of "how do you know?" not so much as an epistemological issue but rather as a recognition that all language of revelation is nevertheless human language, and thus must be judged accordingly; the truth of revelation does not come out of the blue. Logical linguistic analysis thus helps theologians explore the misuse of theological language (1975b: 36).

Although he draws on these three types of linguistic analysis, Schillebeeckx is also critical of them all, for "they all begin with a methodological reduction, that is, they place the reality of what is meaningfully said between brackets. We must therefore have recourse to a form of linguistic analysis in which reality itself is brought in" (1975b: 37). The reality or the ontological aspect of language can be summarized in a sentence: "Language is therefore essentially a medium of revelation" (1975b: 39). Language reveals being. But being is the condition of the possibility of language. Correcting Bultmann's purely existential interpretation of scripture, and countering the assertion of the "linguisticality of reality," Schillebeeckx argues that revelation has a similar structure to that of the verbal event, in that in revelation someone reveals something to someone else. "In other words, revelation and interpretation are correlative, and no historical event can be a decisive act of God for us unless we accept and understand it as something that determines our understanding of ourselves and of reality" (1975b: 40).

5.4.2 *Criteria for Truth: Theological Criteria*

Schillebeeckx begins his discussion of truth by noting: "There is at present such pluralism in faith and in moral concepts that many different 'fronts' have been formed, cutting across the frontiers of the various churches" (1975b: 45). Thus, in the light of this pluralism of faith, truth cannot be understood as unchanging propositions or as ahistorical and non contextual statements of dogma. Truth in the pluralistic context is what Schillebeeckx calls "right faith": "to consider theologically only this pluralism as a fact which can no longer be ignored and which compels us to reflect seriously about what is habitually known as orthodoxy or 'right faith'" (1975b: 46). The criteria for truth in theological hermeneutics are those that would ensure continuity of the orthodox understanding of faith; and "orthodoxy" is not mere reiteration of creedal propositions, for "the demand of 'orthodoxy' consists in full trust in the Biblical Jesus, the Christ in whom the act of salvation of God is accomplished in us" (1975b: 50). The criteria for truth that would ensure the continuity of faith are both theoretical and practical. The theoretical criterion for truth is what Schillebeeckx calls the "proportionate norm." The practical criterion of truth is "orthopraxis." The final criterion is that of acceptance by the people of God. We now turn to a brief analysis of each of these criteria.

5.4.2.1 *The Criterion of the Proportionate Norm*

The criterion of the proportionate norm presumes a plurality of faith experiences, for "a contemporary form of orthodoxy should imply that it is precisely in the plural interpretation of faith that the meaning of God's word of revelation can be heard" (Schillebeeckx 1975b: 60). Clearly, the question arises of how to adjudicate such different interpretations. Schillebeeckx's suggested solution is this: "If the various structures that have arisen in the course of history are compared with each other and, in this comparison, the key words of the Biblical proclamation are taken as a referential framework, we certainly become aware of 'structural rules' which—even if the structure has lost its efficacy in a different social context—still preserve their intelligibility as models for every new structurisation. In this way, we can deduce constant but purely proportional principles which will be a safe guide for our interpretation of faith" (1975b: 61). It may be easier to understand the above passage if we recall Schillebeeckx's understanding of the three planes of history: the ephemeral or fast-moving plane, the conjunctural or slower-moving plane and the structural or slowest- moving plane. Thus, "the various structures that have arisen in the course of history,' of which Schillebeeckx speaks in the above quotation, can be seen as part of the conjunctural plane of human thought and experience. Although these various structures change, there seem nevertheless to be "structural rules" that do not change. Schillebeeckx calls them proportional principles, or norms, which he describes thus: "The norm is therefore proportional, consisting in the relationship between the intentionality of faith and a given (and changing) referential framework" (1975b: 61-62). Again, the referential framework can be seen as part of the conjunctural history, and the intentionality of faith as part of the structural history.

The norm is not a certain articulation of faith; rather, it is the relationship between the message and the context that forms the norm. It is this relationship that forms the continuity in the identity of Christian faith. In other words, "the identity of meaning can only be found on the level of the corresponding relation between the original message and the always different situation" (Schillebeeckx 1989b: 313). Identity of meaning is not a matter of "corresponding terms but corresponding relation of terms" (ibid.). Boff calls the above relationship the "correspondence of relationships" (Boff 1987: 143-50), while Schillebeeckx calls it the "proportionate norm."

This whole notion of the proportionate norm may become clearer if we look at an example from Schillebeeckx's later work (1990:42):

Jesus' message		New Testament message
his social-historical context	=	social-historical context of the NT
Is produced, for example, in the relationship		
Patristic understanding of faith		medieval understanding of faith
its social-historical context		its social-historical context
Which must be produced in the following relationship:		
The present understanding of faith in the year 1990		
Our social-historical & existential context in 1990		

The above hermeneutical method, which utilizes the "correspondence of relationships" or proportionate norm, is in contrast to another hermeneutical method in which the correspondence is on the level of terms. According to this method, if we are identified with Jesus and if our historical context is identified with that of Jesus, then what Jesus did in his time we must do in ours. Thus, we imitate every last detail of Jesus' action without actually giving much attention to the historical context. On the other hand, in the "correspondence of relationships," the identity of meaning is on the level of the relationship of the message to the context. It is the relationship of the terms to each other that constitutes the norm. Thus, in the "correspondence of terms" we imitate the letter, while in "correspondence of relationships" we imitate the spirit.

In other words, the hermeneutical task is not strictly the method of correlation along the lines of Tillich. Schillebeeckx is not attempting to correlate the questions of contemporary men and women with the answers given in the New Testament. Tillich's return to the sources is a way of elucidating the answers that are in the Gospels and making them more understandable to contemporary men and women.[5] By contrast, Schillebeeckx

---

5 Schillebeeckx's (1975b: 85-90) critiques Tillich's method of correlation on two levels:
  1. it confuses two language games by seeking a religious answer to a secular question;
  2. the locus of revelation remains the past, where one seeks the answers to present-day questions.

goes back to the sources to identify those interpretive frameworks that led to a particular articulation and experience of
grace. He further attempts to identify the unitive element in
these experiences, namely, that which is common to these experiences and which holds them together. However, his primary
purpose is not to make those experiences reasonable or understandable to contemporary men and women (even though that
may be a step in the process). Rather, his emphasis is on how revelation occurs *now* and is mediated in contemporary experiences. Thus, he recognizes that there is a proportionality
between Jesus' message and his historical cultural context on the
one hand, and contemporary understanding of faith and the
contemporary historical context on the other. And so, the
hermeneutical task is not only that of making past experiences
and articulations of revelation meaningful in the contemporary
context; it is also one of seeing how contemporary experience
mediates present revelation, in the same way that experiences in
the past mediated revelation in their own time. Contemporary
people need not be attached to the specific articulations of the
experience of salvation from God in Jesus Christ made by first-
century believers or by believers from other eras. Salvation *now*
will be *experienced, understood* and *articulated* differently than it
was in New Testament times. The unitive element that is continuous and that constitutes the continuity between New
Testament times and our own is the experience of salvation from
God in and through Jesus Christ and not any particular articulation or understanding. In this way, Schillebeeckx's hermeneutics
is not strictly linear but rather proportional.

5.4.2.2 The Criterion of Orthopraxis

For Schillebeeckx, theological hermeneutics is not simply an
intellectual exercise, for part of theological hermeneutics is an
interpretation of the future and thus an actualization of God's
promise. He writes, "The object of Christian faith is, of course,

already realized in Christ, but it is only realized in him as our promise and our future. But the future cannot be theoretically interpreted, it must be done" (Schillebeeckx 1975b: 66). This future is salvation and liberation for all men and women, and so the actualization of God's promise is the praxis of liberation for all men and women, seeking the threatened *humanum*. "The humanum which is sought, but always threatened, is proclaimed and promised in Jesus Christ. The kingdom of God is the humanum which is sought, but now promised in Christ, made conceivable and really assured for us in grace" (1975b: 65). Here, negative experiences of contrast have a major critical power (Schillebeeckx 1979: 621-25).

Accordingly, the criterion for the truth of interpretation has to be orthopraxis. Such interpretation results from a critical attitude towards the present situation of oppression of the *humanum* and as a result contains the imperative to change. Only as this happens are we open to the "truth" and only then can the "truth" be made universal. According to Schillebeeckx, "the salvation that is founded in Christ as a promise for all becomes universal, not through the mediation of an abstract, universal idea, but by the power of its cognitive, critical and liberating character in and through a consistent praxis of the kingdom of God" (1990: 176). It becomes clear from the above that Schillebeeckx believes that orthopraxis is not simply an application of a theory, truth or correct interpretation.[6] Rather, orthopraxis is constitutive of faithful interpretation. "This universal liberating praxis is not a secondary superstructure upon, or merely a consequence of, a theoretical truth already recognized as universal, but it is the historical mediation of the manifestation of truth as universal truth, applying to all men and women" (Schillebeeckx 1990: 175). Orthopraxis is constitutive of faithful interpretation of Christian faith, because only in the praxis of liberation can the promise of God be made actual in our time.

---

6 The constitutive relationship of theory and praxis is an insight Schillebeeckx takes from Jürgen Habermas; see Schillebeeckx 1975b: 102-56.

5.4.2.3 The Criterion of Acceptance by the People of God

The final criterion for faithful interpretation is acceptance by the church. Theological hermeneutics or the faithful interpretation of faith is a communal endeavour and has communal ramifications. Moreover, the theologian is not an individual theologizing in a vacuum; rather, he or she is reflecting in and for a community. "The world of faith is a communal world, with a sphere of shared interest and also a world of shared speech and understanding—a 'universe of discourse'. . . . The subject sustaining the hermeneutics is not an individual theologian, but the community of the church as a whole" (Schillebeeckx 1975b: 70).

5.5 The Authority of New Experiences

One might ask the question: if God's revelation is dependent on human experience, does it then follow that God's authority which grounds faith is coincident with human authority? In other words, "If we allow so much room to human experience as a communication of divine revelation, it might be asked: what is left of 'faith from hearing' (Rom. 10.14,17)? Everything—though not in the pre-critical sense of blind faith in an external authority" (Schillebeeckx 1980b: 61).

Revelatory experiences or experiences of faith draw their authority not from the human subject but from God who is revealed in them, although dialectically rather than directly. Even though these experiences are human experiences, their authority derives indirectly from God. "Religious faith is faith 'on the authority of God' and not on the authority of human projections. If experience—both everyday experience and 'scientific' experience'—consists in a dialectical movement of drafting, observing and criticizing the outline through the resistance it offered to by reality, the authority of God is revealed precisely in the fact that the course he takes differs from that of our human plans" (Schillebeeckx 1980b: 61-62).

It is the resistance of God in revelatory experience that diverts and changes the course of human plans, and in this dialectical movement within experience authority is revealed. "The authority of experiences will reveal itself in a *dialectical* appeal to experience" (Schillebeeckx 1980b: 36). In other words, it is God who is the source of the authority which is revealed in "the critical and productive force — the authority — of experience" (1980b: 37).

This kind of authority is not in opposition to the authority of tradition and scripture. Tradition is the repository of the church's collective experiences, and so there can be no question of or reason for splitting experience and tradition. Schillebeeckx writes: "Experiences which are handed down — tradition — are at the same time a means of objectifying new experiences and integrating them in what has already been attained. Experience is traditional experience: experience and tradition are not therefore opposite *per se*: they make one another possible" (1980b: 38). New experiences are only possible in and through tradition, for tradition furnishes the interpretive framework within which new experiences of faith are possible. Tradition, moreover, can be transmitted only through experience.

With respect to the authority of the Bible, Schillebeeckx makes a similar argument. He proposes that the New Testament is best seen as "the Christian interpretation of what had been people's experience with Jesus and was still their experience in the local Christian communities" (1979: 57). Thus, the authority of the Bible stems from the fact that it is the record of the experiences of the people of God, the depository of the Jesus movement. In Schillebeeckx's words, "In that sense, as the Church's 'charter' or foundation document, there can be no substitute for the New Testament's authority" (1979: 58-59). Thus, again, there is no need to split experience and the Bible.

In summary, the authority of revelatory experiences comes from God, who is revealed dialectically in its critical and productive force. Tradition and the Bible are experiences that are handed down through the generations and that make possible contemporary experiences since they act as interpretive frameworks for those new experiences.

5.6 Context and Tradition

For Schillebeeckx, the source of theological reflection and the locus of revelation is human experience. However, this living source has two poles: experiences of previous generations of the church, which he calls "tradition"; and the contemporary experiences of today, which he calls "situation." One cannot seek to reflect theologically on one pole without the other, for tradition is constitutive of contemporary experience and contemporary experience is the vehicle through which tradition is transmitted. So, "What was experience for others yesterday is tradition for us today. . . . However, what once was experience can only be handed down in renewed experiences, at least as living tradition. . . . This already means that Christianity is not a message which has to be believed, but an experience of faith which becomes a message" (Schillebeeckx 1981b: 50).

Thus, the method that Schillebeeckx is advocating is a back-and-forth movement between those two poles, the contemporary situation and tradition. This movement is, however, *critical*. As Schillebeeckx puts it in the *Interim Report*, "The third hinge on which the two Jesus books turn is connected with the critical correlation between the two sources of theology. . . . on the one hand the tradition of Christian experience and on the other present-day experiences" (1981b: 50). What does the critical correlation between situation and tradition entail? "What we are concerned with is rather a mutually critical correlation in which we attune our belief and action within the world in which we live, here and now, to what is expressed in the Biblical tradition. This correlation therefore requires: 1. an analysis of our present world or even worlds of experience; 2. an analysis of the constant structures of the fundamental Christian experience about which the New Testament and the rest of the Christian tradition of experience speak, and 3. the critical correlation and on occasion the critical confrontation of these two 'sources'" (1981b: 50-51). The mutual critical correlation entails an analysis of our present-day situation that cannot ignore experience of meaninglessness, but that also needs to reflect on experiences of meaning, such as the action of some to alleviate experiences of suffering. It also entails looking at the historical and social situations of the particular era in which we are interested, analyzing its world views, philosophy and language. Only then can we identify those unitive structures or proportionate norms that can guide us in our contemporary interpretation. Only then can we put this "critical correlation into practice" (1981b: 60) and thus make actual God's kingdom.

It is this kind of procedure that Schillebeeckx follows in his christological writings. He starts from an analysis of the New Testament experience of grace, which entails an analysis of the socio-historical situation, the language and its use at that time, and the theological and philosophical culture of the time, since the experience of grace is a dialectical unity of all the above. From this, Schillebeeckx identifies a thread that seems to be common to all the different New Testament experiences of grace. However, the analysis is done with the present situation in mind. Schillebeeckx's concern in our present situation is the question of meaninglessness, whether on the intellectual level or on the level of suffering and poverty. In the process, he attempts to arrive at an interpretation of the Jesus event that is faithful to the biblical experiences and that is relevant to our present situation. We now turn to a detailed analysis of Schillebeeckx's christological writings.

6

JESUS THE CHRIST

6.1 The Role of Experience

This chapter will explore the way in which Schillebeeckx's understanding of experience shapes his christology. From the previous chapters in this section, one can see that for Schillebeeckx experience is important for two intrinsically connected reasons. On the one hand, experience is the medium of revelation, that is, there is no revelation without experience. On the other hand, because we simply cannot understand what we do not experience, hermeneutical issues of faithful interpretation of Christianity in history are central.

On the level of the relationship between experience and revelation, Schillebeeckx believes that the Jesus movement started with experience, namely, the experience of the encounter with Jesus. The basis for a reflection on Jesus Christ, i.e., christology, is the experience of the encounter with Jesus. Schillebeeckx writes: "It began with an encounter. . . . This astonishing and overwhelming encounter with the man Jesus became the starting-point for the New Testament view of salvation. To put it plainly, 'grace' has to be expressed in terms of encounter and experience. . . . Furthermore, this means that any further reflection on the meaning of grace and salvation must always go back to the original 'source experiences' without which any theology of grace soon turns into mythology and ontology (in the pejorative sense)" (1980b: 19). The revelation of God in Jesus Christ was perceived as such only because it was experienced as such.

The second issue, concerning the importance of experience in regard to hermeneutics and the faithful interpretation of our faith, has to do with what is constant within the changing. In Schillebeeckx's words, it is the search for "the constant unitive factor" in all faithful interpretations of Christ, whether within the New Testament, in the Councils or through history up to our times (1979: 52). Schillebeeckx rejects several solutions to this search. The unitive factor is not found in the New Testament Gospels, because of diverse christologies are available there. It is not to be found in the "gospel within the gospel," because that criterion is subjective. Nor is it in the "oldest pictures of Jesus," for these may be neither the richest nor the most subtle. The unitive factor cannot be found in "Jesus' own self-awareness" for Jesus' self-awareness is also mediated through the experience of the disciples and the church. Furthermore, the unitive factor cannot be the "sayings and acts of Jesus," for those also are a matter of choice by the community. Finally, the unitive factor cannot be "creedal statements," for some creeds persist and others disappear according to cultural change (1979: 53-55). Rather, the unitive factor in the authentic interpretation of Christ is "the Christian movement itself. In other words a Christian oneness of experience which does indeed take its unity from its pointing to the one figure of Jesus, while nonetheless being pluriform in its verbal expression or articulation. . . . The constant factor here is that particular groups of people find final salvation imparted by God in Jesus of Nazareth" (1979: 56). The "unitive factor" is what Schillebeeckx would call "fundamentally identical experience [which] underlies the various interpretations to be found throughout the New Testament: all its writings bear witness to the experience of salvation in Jesus from God" (1980b: 463). Put differently, the experience of salvation in Jesus from God is the source experience for all the other experiences. Thus, the experience of salvation from God in Jesus is a first-order assertion that has to be maintained in authentic and faithful interpretation of Jesus. Reflections on the identity of Jesus are second-order reflections that are coloured by different interpretive frameworks. So

Schillebeeckx asks: "If we should affirm our belief that in Jesus God saves human beings ('first-order assertion'), how then are we to understand Jesus himself, in whom God's definitive saving action has become a reality ('second-order assertion')?" (1979: 549).

A question arises here, however. If Schillebeeckx claims that there are different experiences of Christ precisely because of the different interpretive frameworks such as philosophy and world view, how can he speak of the "unitive factor" in all interpretations as an "identical experience" (1979: 52)? To answer this question, it may be helpful once again to recall his analysis of history (1979: 577-578). In the same way as there are "different planes of history," so also there are different "planes of experience." The "unitive factor" or the "identical experience" that underlies all different experiences of Jesus belongs to the structural plane: the experience of salvation from God in Jesus is a structural element that has undergone no change. The experiences of Jesus as the high priest or the wisdom of God or teacher or pre-existent word all belong to the conjunctural plane of experience. Those experiences change over time precisely because of different interpretive frameworks. However, they all have the same structural element, "the experience of salvation in Jesus from God."

Finally, the importance of experience resides in the fact that Christianity, according to Schillebeeckx, is not a message that is handed down but rather a life to be lived. "Religion is not concerned with a message that has to be believed but with an experience of faith which is presented as a message" (Schillebeeckx 1980b: 62). In other words, our faith is handed down through experience.

In summary, experience is important for christology for several reasons. On the theological level, there is no revelation without experience; on the hermeneutical level, we cannot understand revelation without experience; and, finally, experience is the link that, ensures the continuity and identity of the Christian faith. What ensures identity is the unitive experience of salvation from God in Jesus Christ which is experienced differently in every age and time. How do we gain access to the experience articulated in the New Testament?

6.2 The Centrality of the Historical Jesus

Our only access to the experience of the disciples, the early church and Jesus is through historical research. Thus, the importance of historical research is not that it proves the tenets of faith; rather, it is a tool that brings us closer to the man Jesus whom we claim to follow. This is why Schillebeeckx disagrees with the rejection of the importance of historical research for faith by followers of Bultmann. Schillebeeckx argues that it was reflection on the earthly life and death of the man Jesus of Nazareth that led people to declare him as the Christ. It is Jesus' earthly life, that is, his history, that led to the confession,[1] and our only access to the earthly Jesus is through historical research, even if that research can never be complete. For Schillebeeckx, "Jesus is in fact a historical and therefore a contingent being: his historical career must explain the Biblical expectations and so-called honorific titles and not vice versa, and precisely this is what happens in the New Testament" (1990: 107). In this sense, the historical method ensures that the Christ we claim to follow is not simply a myth or a construction of our imagination, but an appropriate interpretation of the man Jesus of Nazareth. Historical study "gives a concrete content to faith" (Schillebeeckx 1979: 73) and thus becomes "essential for the access of faith to the authentic gospel" (1979: 75), thereby exerting a critical function. Jesus of Nazareth is the norm and criterion of any christology (1979: 43). "Thus Jesus of Nazareth turns out to be, speaking theologically, the constant anti-pole of the Christ-confessing churches, even though this Opposite Presence—criterion and norm—can never be grasped *per se* but only apprehended in the process whereby the Christian churches let themselves be defined by Jesus" (1979: 76).

---

1 Schillebeeckx makes a distinction between the earthly Jesus who lived and died in Palestine, and the historical Jesus who is reconstructed by research (1979: 75).

In summary, the understanding of the importance of the earthly Jesus as norm and criterion of any christology and the resultant importance of historical research are a manifestation of the importance of experience for any reflection on our faith and more specifically for any christology.

6.3 The Letter to the Hebrews

Having set out some of the hermeneutical and methodological underpinnings of Schillebeeckx's christology, we turn to look in some detail at a sample of his christological writing: his interpretation of the letter to the Hebrews, which he himself regards as the best example of what he perceives his method to be (Schillebeeckx 1980b: 292).

Before turning to this specific example, which appears in *Christ: The Experience of Jesus as Lord*, it is important to situate it within the book's general plan. The work is divided into four parts. In the first part, Schillebeeckx discusses the authority of new experiences and the authority of the New Testament. There is a false dichotomy between the authority of new "experiences" and that of the New Testament. This notion follows from Schillebeeckx's belief that revelation is mediated in human "experiences" new and old. In this regard, the method of correlation is important: to understand the New Testament and to make it relevant in our times, we must enter into dialogue with the New Testament in order to recognize the continuity that exists between our questions and "experiences" and the "experiences" of the New Testament people. To enter into dialogue with the New Testament, we ought to know what the New Testament authors are attempting to express and how they say it. This is the function of Part Two of *Christ*.

Part Two, the most important part for our discussion, Schillebeeckx argues that "experience" is a dialectical unity between encounter with reality, thought and language. This is exemplified in his discussion of the New Testament experience of grace, in which he explores how the different concepts of grace have been used and understood not only in the Hebrew Tanach, but also in Hellenistic Greek culture, and moves from there to an analysis of the "New Testament experiences of grace and their meaning." In the chapters dealing with the different authors of the New Testament, he starts by analyzing prevailing philosophies and world views in order to establish a general sense of the context, and then analyzes the specific situation of each particular church. In the light of the language that was available to the authors, the particular interpretive frameworks exemplified in their world views and the particular historical situation they faced, the "experience" of grace can be understood. The various contexts explain the different interpretations of grace and of Jesus Christ in the New Testament.

In Part Three of the book, Schillebeeckx attempts to identify some structural elements of the New Testament theologies of grace. This is in preparation for Part Four, in which he establishes correlation between the structural elements and the contemporary believer, seeking to recognize revelation in our contemporary experience in a parallel fashion to the experiences of earlier times. Thus, it is important for Schillebeeckx to identify unitive elements not only in the New Testament "experiences," but also in our contemporary "experiences."

Let us now turn to Schillebeeckx's interpretation of the letter to the Hebrews. He introduces his discussion by giving us a glimpse of the author of Hebrews, most probably an Egyptian Jew who lived in Alexandria. He had a twofold spiritual background: he was a Hellenist from Alexandria, but he was also a Jew through and through (Schillebeeckx 1980b: 241). In the letter itself, which is thought to be a homily, the author is concerned with two major problems that seem to have been affecting his community. One problem is the fear of apostasy, and the other is the problem of suffering. Thus, the author attempts to articulate what it means to say, in light of this specific historical situation, that salvation comes from God alone in Jesus the Christ. Schillebeeckx writes: "The Christian community to which the author addresses himself is well versed in Greek thought, and the author's sole concern is to articulate the apostolic experience of faith—the experience of decisive and definitive salvation from God in Jesus—in profoundly human expressions from the thought and the life of his environment, against the background of the threat of a considerable apostasy on the eve of a persecution" (1980b: 238).

Schillebeeckx then says something about the social conditions at that time. There had been a break between the synagogue and the church which had resulted in the loss of the Christians' right to practise their faith. This had led to persecution of the Christians and loss of their property. Thus, many people had converted back to Judaism. Another reason for the conversion back to Judaism was the longing of some for the cultic practices of the Judaic priesthood. As a result, the author of Hebrews attempts to convince the Christians in his community that Christianity has a solid basis in Judaism: "So in his work the author seeks to show what it means for Jesus to be the *Christ*, that is (as far as he is concerned), the eschatological priestly Messiah. He seeks to create a solid basis for a proper understanding of this mystery with material from the Tanach. In an unparalleled way he seeks to secure the Jewish basis of Christianity and to show that the Tanach itself intended that the levitical priesthood should have a *provisional* character" (Schillebeeckx 1980b: 240).

Schillebeeckx also describes the philosophical background of the letter to the Hebrews. This community was very much affected by Platonic philosophy as well as by Hellenistic Jewish apocalyptic. "In the Alexandria where the author lived, the pattern of two levels of reality had already been reinterpreted in Hellenistic terms. It had become a visible and transitory world which exists at the same time and over against a *kosmos noetos*, the super-sensible world of ideas (as in Platonism). As a Hellenist the author is familiar with this Greek conception of a two-storey world, but as a Jew (who also has a perfect knowledge of the Septuagint), he is more influenced by the Jewish 'historical' scheme of the 'present world' as compared with a future world, in other words with the pattern of (Hellenistic-Jewish) apocalyptic" (Schillebeeckx 1980b: 241).

In section §1, which is entitled "The cultural and religious presuppositions of Hebrews," Schillebeeckx specifies the world view of the Alexandrian Hellenistic Jews (§1.I). He details how the author of Hebrews understood the coming of Jesus, and the Jewish understanding of history in the light of the Platonic "two-storey world" of the time. In other words, we have three concepts at work here: (1) the special "two-storey world"; (2) the way in which this world is further interpreted in a temporal way because of the Jewish understanding of history; and (3) the way in which Jesus fits into this scheme. Thus, the "first age" or "this world" is under the dominion of angels until the coming of the "Son of man." The "second age" is that identified with Christ and the Kingdom of God. All that is in the "first age" is perishable except that which is of abiding value, such as love and faith, which also belong to the "second age." "God is enthroned above both dimensions of reality" (Schillebeeckx 1980b: 246). "As the great mediator between the first age and the future age, Christ, 'the Son' receives an equal all-controlling position ([Heb.] 1.2; 2.5). As the point of juncture on earth between the two worlds he spans them both, 'appointed (as he is) the heir of all things, through whom he also created the world' ([Heb.] 1.2). Therefore Jesus Christ is not only the point of juncture between the two ages but at the same time the connection between them; he is the bond between what is incorruptible in the world of creation . . . and the essential incorruptibility of the second age" (ibid.).

In section §1.II, Schillebeeckx analyzes the second and strictly religious interpretive framework of the author of Hebrews: Schillebeeckx calls it the "Melchizedek Midrash." Schillebeeckx starts with Hebrews' understanding of Moses. To a Diaspora Jew, Moses was not only the leader of Israel, but also a prophet, a king and a high priest. Jesus Christ, however, is a prophet "greater than Moses." Schillebeeckx then offers an analysis of Melchizedek:

"Hebrews interprets *melek sālēm* (Gen. 14.18, where this refers to a vassal, a king, who is prepared to submit) as king of Salem: king of peace, called Melchizedek, or *melek* of *ṣedeq*, king of righteousness. This etymology serves as a prelude to his Christian interpretation of Melchizedek=Christ, the king of righteousness and peace" (1980b: 248). To say that Jesus Christ is of the order of Melchizedek is not enough, for that is not enough of an incentive to stop apostasy. The author of Hebrews must convince the Christian Jews of Alexandria that to be of the order of Melchizedek implies a higher status than that of the levitical priests. He must also prove his point using the Tanach. According to Schillebeeckx, the author of Hebrews understands Melchizedek to represent the authentic and proper priesthood, which is greater than Abraham and does not descend from the tribe of Levi. Moreover, Jesus Christ, who is a priest after the order of Melchizedek, is higher than the Jewish priests. Thus, "the Jewish, levitical priesthood has a lower status than that of Melchizedek. A priest after the order of Melchizedek is a transcendent order, much higher than Jewish priesthood" (1980b: 249). Furthermore, "the only priest is Jesus. . . . 'After the order of Melchizedek' points to the eternal character of this priesthood, which is thus something from the *oikoumenē mellousa*, the second age or the future world: prepared by God before the creation of the world, appearing in time and made fast for ever in heaven" (1980b: 250).

In section §2, entitled "A priestly conception of grace and salvation," Schillebeeckx attempts to explore the "experience" of salvation in and through Jesus Christ the high priest as this "experience" was understood by the author of Hebrews. In this section, Schillebeeckx focuses on the specific articulation and understanding of the experience of salvation. He also deals with what, in his opinion, is the foundation of the letter to the Hebrews, namely, that Jesus is "from God" and "from man." In section §2.I.A, he establishes that Jesus is the Son and not an angel. Angelology seems to have been widespread in Hellenistic Greek culture. Furthermore, angels, according to the author of

Hebrews, were the directors of the "first age." In Schillebeeckx's opinion, the author of Hebrews is attempting to counter both an "angel christology" and a cult of angels; he is also trying to prove that Jesus Christ is above angels (1980b: 257).

The essence of Hebrews (§2.I.B), according to Schillebeeckx, is the notion of Jesus Christ as high priest. There are two aspects of Jesus' authentic priesthood. One aspect is the faithfulness of Jesus Christ to God; thus, Jesus Christ is "from God." The second aspect is solidarity with suffering humanity, and thus Jesus Christ is "from man." In addition, it seems that, given the understanding of Jesus Christ as the high priest, the author of Hebrews expresses "God's preference for the insignificant and the lowly" (1980b: 257). In sections §2.I.C and §2.I.D, Schillebeeckx continues to examine both the image of Jesus as the eschatological high priest and the understanding of Christ as the high priest. Thus far, Schillebeeckx can say that "Hebrews does not in any way reinterpret Christianity in terms of Judaism. It is more correct to say that it 'demythologizes' the priestly image, current in Judaism and throughout late antiquity, of the pontifical priest. This is made more human by showing how the priest has solidarity with suffering mankind, how God confirms the validity of such a pattern of life, and how Jesus in heaven defends men's concerns before God" (1980b: 260). In section §2.I, Schillebeeckx describes who Jesus is: specifically, Jesus is "from God" and "from man." In section §2.II, "The ministry of the messianic priest Jesus," Schillebeeckx attempts to locate the actions of Jesus that lead to a messianic understanding of him. In section §2.II.A, Schillebeeckx suggests that the author of Hebrews locates Jesus' solidarity with humanity in his crucifixion, thereby combining two traditions—one that understands crucifixion as a sin offering, and the other that understands crucifixion as a covenant sacrifice (1980b: 265). One can see that these two traditions fit neatly with the essence of priesthood. Crucifixion as a sin offering, represents Jesus who is in solidarity with humanity, whereas crucifixion as a covenant sacrifice represents the faithfulness of Jesus to God. The second point, namely, Jesus' faithfulness to God, is discussed by Schillebeeckx in section §2.II.B, where he explores the concept of Jesus as "advocate of man to God: access to God."

In section §2.III, Schillebeeckx discusses the result of the priestly ministry of Jesus. "The result of the ministry of the earthly and heavenly Jesus is salvation from God in and through Jesus, experienced as a unique priest ([Heb.] 7.25). So he is the pioneer of our salvation ([Heb.] 2.10) or 'the cause of eternal salvation' ([Heb.] 5.9 and 10.1-8) by opening up access for us to God" (1980b: 274).

On the basis of God's salvation, the church of God participates in the heavenly liturgy of Jesus (§2.III.A). Furthermore, the church experiences the tension between the "'now already' of hope" (§2.III.B) and the "'not yet' of faith" (§2.III.C).

However, this experience cannot be the end of the story, for an experience of salvation leads to action. Salvation is outward-oriented towards others; it prompts action. This notion is the basis of section §2.IV, which is entitled "Christian spirituality, the consequence of a priestly doctrine of grace." "Not only does Hebrews indicate the ethical consequences of its doctrinal view ([Heb.]10.19-39); in a number of characteristic and well-chiselled sentences it outlines its view of Christian spirituality: 'Let us go forth from the camp' ([Heb.] 13.13), 'to the *"oikoumene mellousa"* ([Heb.] 2.5) or the future world' ([Heb.] 13.14); and 'enter into God's rest' (3.7-4.11)" (1980b: 285). In section §2.IV.A, the spirituality of this particular community is designated as that of an exodus community, which is at the margin and thus is critical of the world around it. However, this community is also one of worship. Furthermore, since the author of Hebrews is dealing with the issue of suffering, another aspect of the community's spirituality is "the rest of God" (§2.IV.B).

So, what has Schillebeeckx accomplished in his interpretation of the letter to the Hebrews? If we may recall, "experience" is a dialectical unity of language, interpretive frameworks and an encounter with reality, all taking place in a particular historical situation. For an understanding of Hebrews, all four aspects of "experience" have to be analyzed. Schillebeeckx starts with the particular historical situation that the church was facing at the time, namely, persecution and apostasy. Apostasy occurred, not only because of persecution, but also because Hellenistic Christian Jews were enamoured of the cultic worship of the Judaic priesthood. Schillebeeckx analyzes the interpretive frameworks prevalent at the time. These included not only the philosophical interpretive framework of Platonism, but also the religious interpretive framework of Hellenistic Jewish apocalyptic. In light of this analysis of philosophy and the interpretive frameworks, Schillebeeckx is in a position to examine the interpreted experience of grace in terms of Jesus the high priest. Schillebeeckx proceeds to explain what was central to this experience, namely, the solidarity of Jesus with humanity and his faithfulness to God to the point of death on the cross. This experience of grace was manifested on two levels. On one level, the church saw itself participating in the heavenly liturgy; it was also better prepared to deal with the tension of the "already" and the "not yet" (in the midst of the process of suffering). On the other level, members of the church were exhorted as a community to have certain attitudes towards each other, exemplified by ethical demands.

Schillebeeckx summarizes his understanding of Hebrews in the following words:

> Hebrews is not a gospel, nor even a letter, but a kind of lecture or homily. However, the author sets out to depict the Christian experience of salvation in Jesus from God in a particular framework of interpretation. Therefore Hebrews is one of the best New Testament examples of the problem presented by the relationship between *experience* and (theological) *interpretation*. The author *experiences* Jesus as *high priest*; for him this is not merely a superstructure which might be seen as extremely successful in relation to the world-view and the religious presuppositions of the author and his audience. It is an experience and an interpretation at the same time, in such a way that we can always understand

> why other New Testament authors experience and interpret
> Jesus otherwise, although each one is aware that it is a ques-
> tion of one and the same Jesus . . . we should again be able
> to experience the same Jesus differently within a new and
> different horizon of experience. (1980b: 292-93)

Thus, one can speak, as it were, of a "basic revelation" whereby
the disciples encountered God's salvation in and through Jesus
Christ. The New Testament writings reveal that this revelation was
interpreted, articulated and, thus, "experienced" differently by different people. Schillebeeckx attempts to "show how all authors [in
the New Testament] as it were colour the same basic experience —
of decisive and definitive salvation from God in Jesus — according
to the horizon of their own experience and understanding, on the
basis of difficulties and problems which arose in the Christian communities to which they wrote their letters or Gospel" (1980b: 112).
The encounter with reality, which was understood as the experience of God's salvation in and through Jesus Christ, is the unitive
element, not only in the New Testament experiences of grace, but
in our contemporary life. However, precisely because of the different horizons and interpretive frameworks, this encounter with
reality is experienced and articulated differently. As a result, contemporary men and women must re-articulate their "experiences"
of God's salvation in Jesus Christ according to their own interpretive framework. This articulation need not be in terms of Jesus
Christ the high priest.

6.4 Elements Common to All Interpretations of Jesus the Christ

From his analysis of the New Testament as a whole,
Schillebeeckx concludes that there are four elements or structures that are common to all the New Testament interpretations
of grace. These structural elements constitute the common thread
in the New Testament experience of salvation from God in Jesus
Christ, and are thus similar to the third "structural" plane of history. If we want to be faithful in our own understanding of Jesus

for our times, these elements must also be present. Schillebeeckx writes: "In the light of all that has gone before, we now arrive at *four structural* elements which Christians must take account of in any contemporary reinterpretation in which an echo of the gospel of Jesus Christ can be detected, if they want to preserve this gospel in its wholeness while at the same time making it speak to their own age in word and deed" (1980b: 638).

The first structural element addresses the issue of God and God's history with humanity. In any faithful interpretation, one cannot go against the premise that God is for humanity and creation is good. In other words, creation is the symbol of God's abiding presence with humanity. God's verdict on creation in spite of suffering and evil is that it is good. In Schillebeeckx's words, "the bitter question, insoluble in human terms, of the meaning and purpose of human life in nature and history, in a context of meaning and meaninglessness, of suffering and moments of joy, has received a positive and unique answer surpassing all expectations: God himself is the guarantor that human life has a positive and significant meaning" (1980b: 638).

The second structural element addresses the centrality of Jesus in the understanding of God's activity. For Christians, any interpretation of the Christian message has to involve Jesus Christ. Although salvation is from God, for Christians salvation is experienced in and through Jesus Christ. In order to understand and see God, the Christian must look at Jesus Christ. In Schillebeeckx's words, Jesus Christ is the "parable" of God (1979: 626). " . . . God, who here shows his own solidarity with his people, their own calling and their own honour, and therefore identifies himself not only with the ideals and visions of Jesus, but with the person of Jesus of Nazareth himself" (Schillebeeckx 1980b: 639). However, Jesus is not only the "parable" which explains God, but also a "paradigm" that leads humanity to a better life, to salvation. In other words, "In Jesus, we have a complete portrayal of both the predestination of God and the meaning of human life: furthering the good and resisting evil" (Schillebeeckx 1980b: 640). Thus, the

second structural element in any interpretation is the christological element. It articulates the christological mediation of salvation
for Christians (Schillebeeckx 1981b: 52).

The third structural element in any Christian interpretation
concerns the Kingdom of God. It is a kingdom that must be
made actual by orthopraxis. It is simply not enough to confess
Jesus Christ as Lord; the crucial step is an active following of
Jesus, for it is through action that the Kingdom of God is made
real here and now. Schillebeeckx writes: "Christian life itself can
and must be a *memorial* of Jesus Christ. Orthodox confession of
faith is simply the expression of truly Christian life as a *memoria
Jesu*. Detached from a life-style in conformity with the kingdom
of God, the Christian confession becomes innocuous and *a priori*
incredible" (1980b: 641). This emphasis on the Kingdom of God
brings out the importance of the community. It is not simply
individual life and salvation that are important, but the life of all.
In this structural element, Schillebeeckx articulates the importance of the church (1981b: 52). "Therefore we can only speak of
the history of Jesus in terms of the story of the Christian community which follows Jesus" (Schillebeeckx 1980b: 642). In this
third element, the Kingdom of God, as a renewed and just
world, is forged when the community follows Jesus' step by
resisting evil. For only in praxis can the Kingdom of God be
made actual in the here and now.

The fourth structural element in any faithful interpretation
of the Christian message is the eschatological element
(Schillebeeckx 1981b: 52). It is the element of promise with God's
relationship to humanity. Again, it is a promise that is made real
in a fragmentary fashion in and through our action. In Paul's
words, it is the "not yet" that exerts a critical force which corrects
our perspectives and actions. "Although the definitive salvation
is eschatological, and as such is obviously not experienced as the
content of present experience, the awareness of this final perspective — the promise — in faith is given in an experience here
and now, namely in fragments of individual experiences of sal-

vation which bear within themselves an inner promise, as was the case in and through Jesus" (Schillebeeckx 1980b: 642).

These theological perspectives, then, form the fundamental structural elements of the experience of salvation and grace from God in Jesus Christ, mediating the articulation of the experience of grace in the New Testament (Schillebeeckx 1980b: 643).

6.5 Jesus the Eschatological Prophet

Schillebeeckx believes that the understanding of Jesus as the eschatological prophet is the common thread in all the New Testament christologies. He writes: "One of the basic arguments in my first Jesus book is that the first Christian interpretation of Jesus in the period before the New Testament was more than probably in terms of the 'eschatological prophet like Moses,' and that this tendency can still be recognized from a variety of early Christian strata in the New Testament" (1981b: 64). From his exegetical work on the New Testament texts, Schillebeeckx believes that Jesus as the eschatological prophet is the "matrix which gave rise to" (1981b: 69) the rest of the New Testament interpretation of Jesus Christ. Furthermore, "the identification of Jesus with the eschatological emissary from God was the bridge between 'Jesus of Nazareth' and the Christ proclaimed by the Church" (Schillebeeckx 1979: 383).

Schillebeeckx believes that the origin of the interpretation of Jesus as the eschatological prophet is the so-called "maranatha or parousia christology." The eschatological prophet thus is derived from the prophetic and apocalyptic tradition in the early church (Schillebeeckx 1979: 405).

For Schillebeeckx, the basic component of the understanding of Jesus as the eschatological prophet is that "Jesus [is] the one who brings the approaching salvation, [who is] Lord of the future and judge of the world" (Schillebeeckx 1979: 405). Jesus is understood as the prophet who brings the definitive message from God. As a messenger he "is significant for the whole history of the world. . . . Thus eschatological prophet means a prophet who claims to bring a definitive message which applies to the whole of history" (Schillebeeckx 1981b: 67). As such, Jesus is "the eschatological bringer of salvation" (Schillebeeckx 1979: 409).

However, this understanding of Jesus as the eschatological prophet who brings definitive salvation from God resulted from Jesus' own lifestyle, in particular from the way he proclaimed the Kingdom of God, the way he lived this belief and the way he died. The notion of eschatological prophet is grounded in the life and death of the earthly Jesus.[2]

The particular aspect of Jesus' life that grounded it was its theocentric focus. This theocentric focus was manifested in his understanding of the Kingdom of God and its praxis as "the saving presence of God, active and encouraging, . . . which takes concrete form above all in justice and peaceful relationships among individuals and peoples" (Schillebeeckx 1990: 111). The Kingdom of God was the way Jesus described the universal love and concern of God for all creation, "unconditional and liberating sovereign love" (ibid.). And the praxis of the Kingdom of God was seen in Jesus' manner of life (Schillebeeckx 1979: 178-218). Jesus was present to those around him, especially those who were excluded, and that presence was experienced as salvation coming from God. "Jesus wants to give hope to those who from a social and human point of view, according to our human rules, no longer have any hope" (Schillebeeckx 1990: 117). That the Lordship of God was beneficent was seen in Jesus' "wonderful freedom to do good," that is, the way he understood the law to be for the good of humans and not the other way around. Furthermore, Jesus' miracles brought healing of spirit and body, another example of the abiding presence of God. Jesus was accessible to sinners and outcasts; his table fellowship with them manifested the loving presence of God to all. In these ways, Jesus manifested "praxis of compassion" (Kuikman 1993: 114). However, Jesus, proclamation of the kingdom was also an invi-

---

2 For a detailed analysis, see Kuikman 1993.

tation to conversion and *metanoia*, in other words, an invitation to renewal of life (Kuikman 1993: 111).

Another way in which Jesus made clear what he meant by the Kingdom of God was through parables. In his parables "Jesus shows that God comes to stand on the side of those who are pushed aside by the 'community which thinks well of itself': the poor, the oppressed, the outcast and even the sinful. But this 'God of the poor and sinners' is not an indulgent God: he lays claim completely to men and women and asks them to follow him with an undivided heart" (Kuikman 1993: 114). The parables had as their focus the Kingdom of God and the God of compassion. They spoke of the inability of individuals to justify themselves in the presence of God, for it is God's compassion that justifies.

However, in a different manner, Schillebeeckx believes that Jesus himself was the parable of God. If one wants to know who God is, one looks at Jesus Christ. For in and through Jesus, his life and death, we come to understand the God whom Jesus proclaimed.

Jesus' capacity to be the parable of God is grounded in his intimate relationship with God. Schillebeeckx believes that this intimate relationship was manifested in Jesus' "*Abba experience.*" In other words, "what Jesus had to say about God as man's salvation springs directly from his personal experience of God, of the reality which in his own, for the time extraordinary, way he referred to as *Abba*" (Schillebeeckx 1979: 652). Jesus' experience of God as *Abba* draws attention to two things. First, according to Schillebeeckx, it is the experience of "being of God" yet other than God (that is, a creature) that constitutes part of Jesus' *Abba* experience. Schillebeeckx puts the assertion in the form of a question: "The christological question then becomes: Can this fundamental, creaturely status, this 'being of God' —common to all human beings and at the same time differentiated according to each individual's own localized and personal profile —be sufficient ground also in Jesus for elucidating his private, certainly highly profiled *Abba* experience?" (1979: 653; see also 256-69). It is

precisely Jesus' humanity that is the ground of his *Abba* experience, and not any claim about his ontological divinity (1979: 260).

Second, Jesus' *Abba* experience emerged from his own negative contrast experience between, on the one hand, hope and faith in the benevolent God who will not allow evil to have the final word and, on the other hand, the abandonment and suffering of himself and those to whom he was ministering. In Schillebeeckx's words, "on the one hand the incorrigible, irremediable history of man's suffering, a history of calamity, violence and injustice, of grinding, excruciating and oppressive enslavement; on the other hand Jesus' particular religious awareness of God, his *Abba* experience, his intercourse with God as the benevolent, solicitous 'one who is against evil,' who will not admit the supremacy of evil and refuses to allow it the last word" (1979: 267).

Furthermore, Jesus' suffering and his *Abba* experience make him not only a parable of God, but also a paradigm of humanity. For Jesus "experienced the depths of human predicament" (Schillebeeckx 1974: 125), but did not lose hope and worked for the Kingdom of God at the expense of his life. As disciples of Jesus, we are asked to imitate Jesus.

Finally, Jesus' death is also a witness to his beliefs. Schillebeeckx believes that "Jesus' whole life is the hermeneusis of his death" (Schillebeeckx 1979: 311). It was in light of his life that the early church interpreted Jesus' death. Schillebeeckx outlines three interpretations: Jesus died as a martyred prophet; Jesus died as part of God's plan to save the world; and Jesus died as an atonement for our sins (1979: 274). All these interpretations of Jesus' death by the early church were made in light of his earthly life (1979: 294).

It is in light of the life and death of Jesus that the resurrection is also interpreted. Schillebeeckx draws our attention to the fact that "the gospels decline to give us an account of the resurrection itself; and so they enable us to consider it, in terms of experience and language, within a story which can be heard and heeded as a message" (1979: 337). According to Schillebeeckx, the underlying

experience of those first disciples was that of conversion from viewing Jesus simply as Jesus to viewing him as Christ, the bringer of salvation from God (1979: 384). This experience of conversion is manifested in a complete and absolute commitment to Jesus the Christ and his cause. This experience of conversion took on eschatological language and used the motif of appearances. Schillebeeckx writes: "Commitment to Jesus was conceived of in the early Church as a 'conversion.' This conversion to Jesus is frequently represented on the lines of the Jewish conversion vision, which in the early Church gradually becomes an 'appearance' accompanied by the motif of a 'commissioning' or 'sending forth'" (1979: 385). To understand the resurrection through the conversion model does not imply that the experience of the resurrection is simply subjective and has no objective basis, for this would run counter to Schillebeeckx's affirmation that a constitutive aspect of experience is an encounter with a reality other than the subject. The resurrection is to be seen as God's vindication of the rejected message, life and person of Jesus, and as an expression of the power of God to bring the dead to life, especially his messenger of salvation. Thus, the resurrection "really is the faith-motivated experience and confession of the power of God that has brought the crucified One to life again" (Schillebeeckx 1979: 397).

We may draw the threads of this discussion together by highlighting three characteristics of Schillebeeckx's christology, which relate to the question of the relationship of experience and christology: it is theocentric, functional and soteriologically based.

It is theocentric because, interpreting Jesus as the eschatological prophet, it finds the focus of Jesus' message and life in the Kingdom of God. What defines Jesus is his relationship to God through the *Abba* experience; the focus of his identity is God Schillebeeckx's christology is functional, as we see clearly in the way in which he interprets honorific titles of Jesus. "All the honorific titles of Jesus, including "Son of God,' are in the first instance functional, are elements within salvation-history — even

in the late sapiential Johannine gospel with its pre-existence idea" (Schillebeeckx 1979: 545-46).The honorific titles are "relational," articulating the relationship between Jesus and God, and Jesus and his people. "All the honorific titles in the New Testament take their direct origin from the experience of salvation from God in Jesus Christ, as a result of which believers saw their lives change" (Schillebeeckx 1990: 123). The titles at no point reflect the ontological divinity of Jesus. Schillebeeckx writes: "Jesus' uniqueness in his relationship to God undoubtedly lies in its unaffected simplicity;. . . . But we cannot build on it an awareness on Jesus' part of some 'transcendent' sonship and still less a Trinitarian doctrine, as has often happened in the exegetical and theological writings deriving therefrom" (1979: 260). Rather, the titles articulate the experience of the early disciples with Jesus.

Finally, Schillebeeckx's christology is soteriological. This is another way of saying not only that Schillebeeckx believes that Jesus' focus was the Kingdom of God and its praxis of liberation and salvation, but also that we must have that same focus. Thus, Schillebeeckx's christology shares with his Jesus the focus of the Kingdom of God and its praxis. This is in contrast to the development whereby the messenger became the message, where the theocentricity of Jesus turned into the christocentricity of the early church (Schillebeeckx 1990: 123).

PART THREE

FREI AND SCHILLEBEECKX:
A COMPARISON

7

DOCTRINAL DIFFERENCES

In the previous two parts, I have presented two different answers to the question of the role of experience in theology and theological method as found in the works of thought Hans Frei and of Edward Schillebeeckx. In this part, I will compare them and contrast them. The comparison will be done on several levels. Since the contention of this book is that one's theological stance shapes one's questions and how one attempts the answers, I will start with the theological stance of both theologians, and specifically their understanding of revelation and mediation. Their understanding of revelation and mediation is, in turn, reflected in the fundamental questions that inform their theology, which will form the second level of comparison. These questions in turn dictate their methods for seeking the answers; hence, the third level of comparison: the methodological. An aspect of theological method is biblical interpretation. Thus, biblical interpretation is the fourth level of comparison. The fifth and final level is a return to doctrine: christology. In short, we proceed in a circular motion, starting with a theological stance that directs method, which in turn results in another theological stance, which again modifies the method, which results once more in a different stance.

7.1 God's Self-Communication

Where and how is God revealed? The two authors have clearly divergent answers. For Schillebeeckx, God is revealed in human history and life. He quotes a little boy's insight: "People are the words with which God tells his story" (1990: xiii). In Schillebeeckx's opinion, the boy's insight is the theme of his book

Church: The Human Story of God. Elsewhere, Schillebeeckx says bluntly, "there can be no revelation without experience" (1980b: 45). In other words, God's activity and revelation are mediated in human experience.[1] The reasons for this mediation are twofold: the first reason is related to the reality of God. Because God is transcendent, God is immanent. "God's transcendence through immanence, and with respect to man (as a personal being) through overwhelming immanence, has a referential character. Please understand me: I am not saying at all that God's transcendence as such stands over against his own immanence in the world (history and human beings) — that is indeed an unthinkable idea; but we are bound to say that God's immanence only permits us a non-divine, creaturely view, in profile, of his transcendence, which after all is not constituted by his immanence in the creature . . . that immanence is more of a free gift" (Schillebeeckx 1979: 631-32). The media that reveal God for us do not exhaust or totally capture God's essence. Schillebeeckx makes this point to emphasize the limited capacity of the created order to reveal God and thus to underline the necessity of mediation, because of the infinity of God and the finitude of the creature.

The second reason for mediation is related to human reality. "The transcending act which God is would be a thing we could not so much as speak of — not even in faith-language — were it not to manifest itself in the interior traffic of our world. . . . For our speaking about God's transcendence has no ground other than our own contingency" (Schillebeeckx 1979: 627). Or, "how can we describe the way in which reality, under the aspect in which it does not enter our consciousness, can still be *thought of* by this consciousness?" (Schillebeeckx 1980b: 56). Since God is totally other than humanity, there is no way that the human person can understand God, or talk about God, unless God is revealed or manifested within human reality. Thus, the mediated character of our knowledge of God is closely related to the "hermeneutical" character of all human knowledge. In other words, humans can-

---

1 Scheffczyk (1984) argues that Schillebeeckx's understanding of the relationship of revelation to experience results in the merging of the authority of revelation with that of experience. That is the case because Scheffczyk sees Schillebeeckx as offering only a subjectivistic interpretation of revelation.

not understand what is beyond the created order if it is not manifested or mediated in that created order.

As we have seen, what connects these two reasons is Schillebeeckx's doctrine of creation. It is first and foremost God's wish that this be the case. God fashioned the human to be a co-creator with God. God also willed that the divine revelation and salvation of others be done in and through humans. In Schillebeeckx's words, "God creates human beings as the principle of their own human lives so that human action has to develop and effectuate the world and its future in human solidarity, within contingent situations and given boundaries, and therefore with respect of both inanimate and animate nature . . . [God] creates human beings with a free human will, freely to develop their own human future, to realize it in contingent, chance and also specific situations" (1990: 230-31).

Revelation is mediated through human experience or, as Schillebeeckx later claims, revelation has a similar structure to that of experience, and has four characteristics: it is an encounter with reality, i.e., God, experienced by believers, interpreted in religious language and expressed in human terms in the dimension of human history (Schillebeeckx 1980b: 78).

The next issue is the content of revelation. What is revealed is that "God is for us" — God who is faithful and pure gift, whose only concern is the human (Schillebeeckx 1979: 229). The human's happiness is a matter of pride to God (Schillebeeckx 1980b: 512). What is revealed about humans is that they have a responsibility to make God's rule actual by resisting evil and being concerned, like God, with the created order.

Finally, the ground for this understanding of revelation is a very positive outlook on creation. It is God who judged creation to be good. The ambiguity and finitude of the created order are not things to be explained away, but rather are what make the created order what it is. Creation is also an unfinished business, which is made actual through human freedom in action.

In the language of Frei, Schillebeeckx espouses a relational understanding of revelation. For Frei, in contrast to Schillebeeckx, revelation is not relational. He critiques the position of relational theologians because of their emphasis on the subjective aspect of revelation to the detriment of God and Jesus Christ. Revelation for Frei is not mediated through human experience. As he puts it in his early exposition of Barth, "The relation of God to man is not a reversible relation. God is not present in history, experience, thought or even 'existence' in such a way that his revelation of himself becomes a relational state. There is no denial of God's relation to man, but its actualism is so pronounced and critical that at no point does it become a 'given' or 'nexus' or 'relational state' which would justify us in speaking about man's relation to God" (1956: 113). "Positively expressed, this means that the relationship of God to man is wholly grounded in God" (1956: 115). What Frei is attempting to safeguard is the sovereignty and freedom of God. God is not a datum of the human or of human experience; likewise, revelation is not an instance of a wider category of human experience, nor does revelation have a similar structure to that of other human experience.

Revelation is the fact that Jesus Christ came, not what he taught nor his significance to us. Revelation is the simple fact that Jesus Christ is. "In him [Jesus Christ] — and in him alone — the concrete and the universal, Bible and transcendental philosophy, immediacy of divine action and indirectness of human knowledge, the object of knowledge and the way of knowledge, the eternal and the temporal are united" (Frei 1956: 461).

Revelation for Frei has four characteristics: it is objective, identical with Jesus Christ, unmediated by human categories, and finally reflects God's freedom. As he observes about Barth, "The three areas in which we have discovered Barth's indebtedness to relationalism even after the break with liberalism — the questions of immediacy, freedom and objectivity in revelation — all are areas of methodological concern. Though this is still true, it is perhaps somewhat less so when we turn to a fourth area, the christocentricity of the doctrine of revelation" (1956: 459).

Frei's understanding of revelation as objective is a direct critique of relational theologians who emphasize the human pole in revelation.[2] According to Frei, relational theologians posit God

2 This is similar to Barth's notion of objective revelation and salvation which are grounded in the freedom of God. See Hunsinger 1991.

and humans as equal partners in the relationship. As a result, talk about God and Jesus Christ is reduced to talk about humans. For Frei, revelation is grounded only in God. "This objectivity [in theology] would confess God to be not an object, but an abiding subject who is always the presupposition of thought and action and never encompassed by them. God is objective in the sense of being over against us and never contained within a relation of thought or consciousness to us" (1956: 206).

The second characteristic of revelation is that it is identical with Jesus Christ. Revelation is the fact that Jesus Christ came and not what he taught or meant for humanity. For Frei, the loss of Christ's identity in our contemporary times is the result of our preoccupation with the subjective pole of revelation, that is, with the question of our reception of revelation. Frei further emphasizes the uniqueness and unsubstitutability of Jesus Christ and thus of Christian revelation. The event of Jesus Christ is a moment only of itself and therefore so is Christian revelation.

The third characteristic of revelation is that it is immediate. This means that revelation is not mediated in human categories of, for example, reason. The human is not the agent of revelation whether in the sending or the receiving of revelation. God is the agent. Revelation is an activity of God from start to finish.[3] Frei insists with Barth "that the nature of God's self-revelation is God's freedom in and through his self-communication and over the recipient mode, in man, of this communication" (Frei 1956: 458).

The fourth characteristic of revelation is that it reflects the freedom and aseity of God and therefore is not dependent on human freedom. In other words, humanity is not an external condition that limits God's freedom. However, God, in God's self, is a God-towards-humans. Again, this is another way of critiquing relational theologians who emphasize the role of humans in revelation.

In summary, for Frei revelation is Jesus Christ, and not his reception, his acceptance nor even his significance for the world.

---

3 This is similar to Barth's notion of miraculous event. See Hunsinger 1991.

The subjective pole of revelation does not play a significant role in Frei's theology of revelation.[4]

From the above, the differences between Schillebeeckx's and Frei's understanding of revelation can be identified. Schillebeeckx has a highly developed theology of grace, while Frei does not (Webster 1992: 130). Frei's interpretation of Jesus and revelation is christocentric, while Schillebeeckx's is theocentric. Because Schillebeeckx allows more room for the activity of grace and thus mediation, human activity plays a more significant role in revelation. Frei's christocentric understanding of revelation, on the other hand, reduces the human element in revelation to a minimum. Although in his later writings, Frei moves towards the community of Christians as the place where the Holy Spirit is witnessed, this concept is not fully developed.

In terms of traditional Trinitarian language, Frei concentrates on Jesus Christ and Schillebeeckx concentrates on the Spirit in their understanding of revelation. Yet it is interesting to note that, while revelation for Schillebeeckx is the activity of God mediated in human experience, the criterion and norm are Jesus Christ. For Frei, on the other hand, while revelation is Jesus Christ, meaning resides in the community's use and understanding of that revelation. This is the realm of the Holy Spirit. So, while each theologian emphasizes one aspect of God's activity, namely, Jesus Christ or the Holy Spirit, the other aspect exerts the needed critical function.

We now move on to our next question: How did those different ways of understanding revelation affect or direct the basic questions that these two theologians raised?

7.2 Differing Contexts

Schillebeeckx is concerned with the fact that Christianity and its belief system have become irrelevant to Christians today. However, this irrelevance is a symptom of a deeper issue, namely, historical consciousness. Schillebeeckx's stress on historical consciousness shapes his theology as *hermeneutical* and

---

4 However, in his later writings, Frei assigns a greater scope and role to the church in identifying the meaning of revelation and in mediating Christ.

apologetic, and also as *ethical* or *praxis-oriented.* He writes: "While preparing a wider study of the subject [the problem of hermeneutics] I will however, touch upon one—in my view, fundamental—aspect of the problem, that of the historical dimension of our existence as believers, the very root of hermeneutics" (1977: 20).

The historical dimension of our lives does not simply affect our understanding of our faith; it affects the very basis of our faith, namely, revelation. Revelation is also historically mediated. There is no haven where truth, even religious truth, is not touched by historical consciousness, characterized by ambiguity, limitedness, relativity and temporality (Jacko 1987: 26). In Schillebeeckx's words, "The content of revelation is never given to us in a pure state, neat, but in the language of faith, which to a certain degree also already includes theological reflection; it is never the pure expression of immediate experiences of faith" (1981b: vii). Thus, Schillebeeckx's task is to make Christian beliefs more understandable. The task, in other words, is a hermeneutical task.

However, the irrelevance is not only experienced on the intellectual level, when Christian beliefs as they have been handed down no longer seem to make sense. There is a second level on which Christianity is experienced as irrelevant: the level of praxis. Schillebeeckx's major concern is the question of evil and suffering in the world (Nijenhuis 1980: 125-40). In the light of war, poverty, disease and oppression, Christianity, if anything, seems to be supporting the status quo, i.e., those in power. Thus, human suffering seems to continue with Christianity's blessing. Schillebeeckx sees his task as one of addressing these concerns from a Christian point of view (Schillebeeckx 1980b: 671-728). The Christian message has to be reinterpreted so that its concern for the marginalized may be retrieved—a concern that has been lost with time. In other words, Schillebeeckx's task is a hermeneutical concern that is praxis-oriented.

However, the concern about evil in the world and the subsequent action to counter it is not related to faith as a theory to its application, where one applies what one believes to the specific situation of evil. The issue is more complicated than that. For Schillebeeckx, as theory is intrinsically related to practice,[5] so orthodoxy is related to orthopraxis: Christian faith is verified in the action to counter evil. "Orthodoxy is at stake in orthopraxis" (Schillebeeckx 1990: 177).

In summary, Schillebeeckx's work is hermeneutically oriented because of his awareness of historical consciousness. Hermeneutics does not simply refer to the quest for understanding, as if understanding were only an intellectual exercise. To understand is to live and act, for understanding and acting are intrinsic to each other, another expression of the relationship of theory and praxis. That is what Schillebeeckx is seeking.

Frei, on the other hand, is concerned primarily with the issue of identity. In his earlier work, his main interest is in Jesus Christ's identity. In his later work, however, another concern also emerges: the identity of the Christian community.

Frei focuses on Christ's identity in explicit contrast to apologetic discussion of Christ's presence, with its concern for the relationship of Christ to the Christian believer. In his words, "At the outset, I should like to raise two questions. First, why should we talk about the relation between Christ and believers in terms of Christ's presence and identity? Second, why should we talk about it at all, if we are offering neither dogmatic theology nor a rational argument for the truth of Christianity?" (1967: 1-2). Frei distinguishes between two kinds of theology: dogmatic and apologetic on the one hand, and confessional on the other hand. Frei thinks of himself as engaging in confessional theology whose concern is not the relationship of Christ to Christians but rather "the basic conviction itself, that Christian faith involves a unique affirmation about Jesus Christ, viz., not only that he is the presence of God but also that knowing his identity is identical with having him present or being in his presence" (1967: vii). It is only this kind of theology that prevents a dissolution of Jesus' identity. Frei writes:

---

5 The insight on the relationship of theory and practice is from J. Habermas 1990a.

> If one begins with presence rather than with identity, the
> question, How is Christ present? is finally answered by the
> mysterious movement of Christ toward us, coinciding with
> our movement toward him. The result of this complete coin-
> cidence or simultaneity is, in the last analysis, the ultimate
> dissolution of both our own presence and his. His presence
> is not his own; indeed, he is diffused into humanity by
> becoming one with it. And we, in turn, find in him the mys-
> terious symbol expressing our own ultimate lack of abiding
> presence and identity. . . . Such a presence, e.g., that of the
> archetypal and nameless human stranger, and our own
> become mysteriously diffused into each other, so that they
> are one and the same. This, of course, is not what Christians
> believe. (1967: 86-87)

If apologetic concerns dominate, then talk about Jesus Christ
and God becomes talk about our humanity, and Jesus Christ
becomes the symbol of our humanity instead of the "unsubstitutable" person that he is.

But Frei may also be concerned with Christian identity. In his
later work, Frei sometimes expresses the conviction that
Christians are losing their language and culture as Christianity
disappears into the wider culture of the Western world. "The status of Christianity in the modern West has been ambiguous: it
has been viewed and has viewed itself both as an independent
religious community or communities and as an official or at least
privileged institution in the general cultural system, including
the organization of learning and of thinking about the meaning
of culture" (Frei 1992: 1). Christianity and Christians are going
through an identity crisis, not knowing whether they draw their
identity from within their faith system, or from the wider spectrum of culture. "This ambiguity is reflected in two very different, often contentious, but not necessarily mutually exclusive
views of Christian theology" (Frei 1992:1-2). In the first view, it
is the wider culture exemplified in the discipline of philosophy
that sets the norms and criteria. The Christian community is
more and more being swallowed up by the surrounding culture.
In this view, "*Christian* theology is an instance of a general class

or generic type and is therefore to be subsumed under general criteria of intelligibility, coherence, and truth that it must share with other academic disciplines" (Frei 1992: 2). In the second view of Christian theology, norms and criteria are drawn from the belief system. "*Theology* is an aspect of Christianity and is therefore partly or wholly defined by its relation to the cultural or semiotic system that constitutes that religion. In this view theology is religion-specific. . . . In this view theology is explained by the character of Christianity rather than vice versa" (ibid.).

In an ironic parallel, as Christ's identity is lost when the concern is to make him present in our time in and through our experience of him, likewise our identity is lost when our sole concern is our presence to our own times, exemplified in regard for our experience. Thus, Christ's identity and ours are lost.

Again, the solution is to move away from dogmatic and apologetic theology towards confessional theology, exemplified in Frei's second view of theology. He writes, "Here Christian theology is first of all the first-order statements or proclamations made in the course of Christian practice and belief. But second . . . it is the Christian community's second-order appraisal of its own language and actions under a norm or norms internal to the community itself. This appraisal in turn has two aspects. The first is descriptive: an endeavor to articulate the 'grammar,' or 'internal logic,' of first-order Christian statements. The second is critical, an endeavor to judge any given articulation of Christian language for its success or failure in adhering to the acknowledged norm or norms governing Christian use of language" (1992: 2). Our identity is made manifest in our unique belief in Jesus Christ that we hold in our religious system and our unique faith language. To preserve our identity is to be able to use our language fluently, not to explain its truth claims or how we came upon them.

At what point can we discern a contrast between these two questions: the question of relevance and the question of identity. Schillebeeckx's hermeneutical task, which is undergirded by a theology of grace, namely, the universal love of God, gives priority to what is common or universal, and so gives weight to anthropology. Frei, on the other hand, stresses the identity of

Jesus Christ and our Christian identity. Thereby he seeks what is different, specific or "particular,"[6] what he calls the "unsubstitutable." This emphasis on difference permeates Frei's whole enterprise at both the methodological and theological levels.

This, of course, does not mean that Schillebeeckx is not interested in the question of the identity of the Christian community or of Jesus Christ, nor does it mean that Frei is not interested in the question of how to make sense of Christian belief. But it does mean that they have different primary concerns. We now turn to look at how the specific questions of Schillebeeckx and Frei direct their methodology.

7.3 Methodological Considerations

7.3.1 The Specific Way to Address Each Question

The fundamental questions that are raised by Schillebeeckx and Frei guide their methodologies and each theologian's method is specific to the question.

Schillebeeckx's concern is primarily hermeneutical, and this concern is undergirded by a theology of grace, in which God's love is universal and open to all. Therefore, Schillebeeckx's interest is in what is shared by or common to humanity, so that the common experience of humanity is basic in his theology. More specifically, Schillebeeckx is concerned with the question of evil in the world. Hence, for him, the most appropriate starting point for theological reflection is negative experiences of contrast. As a result, the experience of contrast is the context in which he understands the experience of salvation in Jesus from God. In his words, "The striking thing about this process of calamitous and also partly benign experiences is that the distinctive ideas a people have about 'salvation' attempt to probe and interpret, not only the depth and unbounded extent of calamity, suffering, evil and death, endured and enduring, but also their causes, origin and effects. Where salvation is hoped for, it is in the express form of this expectation that evil and suffering are unmasked: in it both are put on exhibition. . . . They look for mercy and compassion at the very heart of reality, despite every contrary experi-

---

6 This is similar to Barth's notion of the particular; see Hunsinger 1991: 32-71.

ence" (1979: 20). That, in summary, is Schillebeeckx's project, namely, how we can talk about God's salvation in and through Jesus in the present time when evil still prevails. The method that he follows seeks to take full account of those experiences. In essence, then, his method is experientially based because of a certain theological stance and a particular question.

Frei, on the other hand, is interested in the question of identity, whether it is the identity of Jesus Christ or the identity of the Christian community. In his earlier work, *The Identity of Jesus Christ*, his interest is in the identity of Jesus as an unsubstitutable person. This unsubstitutability exerts a christological control over or imposes a proviso on his method. To understand the identity of the unsubstitutable Jesus Christ, one cannot use a method that is used for other purposes, for to do so would assume that the identity of Jesus Christ is an instance in a wider category. In other words, as the identity of Jesus is unique, an instance of itself, so must be the method to identify it. The method cannot be the same as other methods or theories. It has to be either unique or very simple, such that one cannot call it a method in the usual sense of the word. Hence, Frei seeks a method that will not overwhelm or eclipse the story of Jesus. This is exemplified in the kind of questions one raises about Jesus Christ, which must be "formal questions." Frei explains that, "before we proceed we need to ask again what is meant by a 'formal question' and why it matters so much for our enterprise. A formal question, such as 'Who is he?' or 'What is he like?' is one to which an answer is necessary if we are to know anything at all about a person. But more importantly, it is a question that will not force an answer that would risk overwhelming either the person or the story" (1967: 89). This is in contrast to two other ways of asking the question about who and what Jesus is. One example will be sufficient to illustrate the point.

One of those ways raises the question about Jesus' identity in the context of his relationship to us. "One approach involves asking how a person in a story illuminates, or perhaps merely illustrates, this or that problem of our common existence" (Frei 1967: 89). In such an approach, a theory about us, such as our existential concerns of alienation and self-estrangement, emerges, and it is to this theory that Jesus has to relate. As a result, the theory about ourselves becomes the primary concern and not Jesus' identity. In Frei's words, "in this instance the category in terms of which the identity question is framed materially influences the answer, and the description is not a formal one. The *question* rather than the story becomes the governing context with which the person is identified" (ibid.). According to Frei, Paul Tillich and Rudolf Bultmann are typical of theologians who fall into this particular trap: existential philosophy becomes the lens through which the answer to Jesus Christ's identity can be perceived, with the result that Jesus Christ becomes a symbol of our existence, and his particularity is swallowed up in his universal symbolic power.

The method Frei is advocating is a method that is similar to the "formal question" he applies to understanding who or what Jesus is. It is a "formal method" whose content would not overwhelm the identity of Jesus Christ, so that his identity can emerge whole and unsubstitutable. Who Jesus is is identical with his actions, that is, his identity is manifested in what he does. However, what Jesus does or what his actions are can be found only in the biblical narrative, read according to its literal meaning. A literal reading of the biblical narrative represents a "formal method" that would not overwhelm the identity of Jesus Christ, and as a result guards the particularity of Jesus' identity. Of course, in this "formal method," which preserves the unsubstitutability of Jesus, Frei does make ad hoc use of other methods and disciplines, for example, the approaches of Ryle and Auerbach.

What method does Frei advocate as he moves into an exploration of the identity of the Christian community? In a similar vein, the method has to be "formal" so that it does not overwhelm the Christian community's identity. To start with, Frei believes that Christianity "is first of all a religion. It is not a network of beliefs, it is not a system, first of all. It may be an intellectual system also, but not in the first place. Further, it is not first of all an experienced something, an experienced shape, an essence. Rather, it is first of all a complex, various, loosely held, and yet really discernible community with varying features—a religious community of which, for example, a sacred text is one feature" (1992: 12). Because Christianity is really a Christian community, the closest analogy to it is culture. Frei, following Clifford Geertz, suggests that "rather than *explaining* the culture one looks at, one tries to *describe* it" (ibid.). Frei is engaging in what I would call a phenomenology of the culture of Christianity. Again, this exercise in *describing* the Christian community does not overwhelm the identity of the community, unlike an attempt to *explain*, which involves a theory about culture and human beings that may overwhelm the description of the Christian community. In describing the Christian community, one emphasizes the "particular" which gives the community its special flavour, rather than attempting to establish the conditions of the possibility of its identity.

In summary, Schillebeeckx's question, which is hermeneutical in outlook, results in a method that seeks the common ground; thus, anthropology or more precisely a theological anthropology, will be his route. Frei, on the other hand, seeks the identity of Jesus Christ and later the identity of the Christian community; as a result, his method emphasizes the particular.

The next question, then, is what the role of theology is in light of these methods and questions.

7.3.2 *The Role of Theology*

For Schillebeeckx, theology exerts a hermeneutical and critical function. The hermeneutical task can be put in traditional words: faith seeking understanding. What does our faith mean for us today? How can we live it? How does our faith relate to other faiths? How can we dialogue with others of different faiths? The critical task is related to the hermeneutical one. The critical task is to uncover misinterpretations and ideologies that negate our faith and run counter to its basic tenets. The critical task must be to ask the question about action and praxis. Theology seeks to understand faith in order to live it.

But precisely because of the nature of the questions and concerns, Schillebeeckx fits Frei's description of an apologetic theologian. The question of understanding and living by faith can be viewed as an anthropological question. To understand faith and to be able to uncover misinterpretations and misleading ideologies, one must look at the condition of the possibility of understanding. The question of how we relate to other faiths must uncover that which is common to both so as to allow dialogue and understanding to take place.

Frei's theology can be labelled confessional, in the sense that he does not seek to explain why his faith takes this or that particular shape or attempt to explain why other faiths take different shapes. Understanding one's faith, for Frei, is not knowing how it started, or why it started, or delving into the condition of its own possibility. Rather, understanding one's faith is being able to use it, just as understanding a language is being fluent in it. Frei is concerned with the *description* of the specificity of his faith. "To learn the language of the Christian community is not to undergo a profound 'experience' of a privileged sort, but to learn to make that language one's own, in faith, hope, and love" (Frei 1992: 54). Thus, Frei's concern is not to understand by explaining; rather, to understand is to know how to use. If that is the case, then the next question is: How do other disciplines relate to theology?

7.3.3 The Relationship of Theology to Other Disciplines

Because, for Schillebeeckx, theology exerts both a hermeneutical and a critical function, there is a need to turn to the expertise of other disciplines to assist theology in its task. Thus, Schillebeeckx turns to philosophy, psychology, sociology, natural sciences and so forth in an attempt to understand humanity, since that is his concern. Schillebeeckx makes most use of the discipline of philosophy. Schreiter describes the different philosophies that Schillebeeckx uses: "The explicit Thomistic framework, developed and used since his contacts with De Petter in the 1930s, was set aside. . . . Rather, his thought shows evidence of a variety of different interpretive frameworks. It was also during this period that he undertook an intensive study of different systems of interpretation: the 'new hermeneutics' of the neo-Heideggerians, Anglo-American analytic philosophy, and the critical theory of the Frankfurt school of social criticism. All of these theories, plus a few others, were to play a role in his subsequent thought" (1984: 5). However, the turn to other disciplines is grounded in a deep trust in God, who is revealed in all human achievements even if they are not clothed in strictly religious language. In Schillebeeckx's words, "not to lose faith in man in all his activities, despite all evil experiences, reveals itself, on close analysis, as a latent, unconditional trust in God" (1977: 77).

Schillebeeckx does not feel obliged to accept all the presuppositions of these disciplines. He simply makes use of their insights in his theology. The relationship is correlative. Insights from other disciplines can perform a critical and corrective function in his theology and vice versa, as can be seen in the example of Schillebeeckx's use of critical theory. Schillebeeckx is willing to accept the critical theorists' insight into the relationship between theory and praxis, and the insight into the ideology within any thought system. However, he refuses to accept radical negativity that may result in an attitude of pessimism towards life. He writes: "We must now consider the radical critical negativity connected with critical theory. . . . It has, however, always been my aim to stress the fact that these negative dialectics are sustained by a positive sphere of meaning which will direct praxis" (1975b: 127). Adorno's negative dialectic does not have the last word, because the power of the negative dialectic can be seen only in contrast to positive meaning. Meaning and not meaninglessness (or, in theological language, God and not evil) has the final word.

Another example of the way in which Schillebeeckx works with other disciplines is his attitude towards linguistic philosophers. Schillebeeckx accepts the insights presented by linguistic philosophers: structural linguistic analysis exposes ideology in language by emphasizing that meaning is contextual, and thus there can be no generalizations in theological language; phenomenological linguistic analysis draws attention to the triadic structure of the verbal event and its communicative ability; logical linguistic analysis addresses the issue of meaningfulness and draws attention to the careless use of language that leads to false questions and problems. However, for theological reasons Schillebeeckx offers a corrective to their insights: "They all begin with a methodological reduction, that is, they place the reality of what is meaningfully said between brackets. We must therefore have recourse to a form of linguistic analysis in which reality itself is brought in" (1975b: 37). Those philosophers of language, in Schillebeeckx's opinion, ignore reality and put on hold the ontological aspect of language. Theologically, one cannot ignore the issue, for the ontological aspect of language claims that what we experience in and through language is an objective reality which is the condition of our possibility. "Language is therefore essentially a medium of revelation" (1975b: 39). Language reveals being. But being is the condition of the possibility of language. In revelation, that reality is God.

Nevertheless, for Schillebeeckx other disciplines provide a corrective to theology. These insights from philosophy, social sciences and sciences not only helped Schillebeeckx to understand his faith better, but also served to reorient his interests and his understanding. Schreiter gives the example of secularization and its effects on Schillebeeckx's work: "There was a marked shift in perspective. The effect of renewal within the church and the forces of secularization outside it meant that the more churchly assumptions and tone of his earlier theology were less feasible to maintain" (1984: 5). The shift in perspective of which Schreiter speaks can be seen in the following example. Schillebeeckx's understanding of the structure of experience affected his understanding of the christological titles. His understanding shifted from understanding those titles as referring to ontological realities to seeing those titles more as relational and functional. Another example of the shift in perspective can be seen in Schillebeeckx's stance on the importance of orthopraxis. In more recent work, orthopraxis is no longer understood by Schillebeeckx as simply an application of orthodoxy, but rather as constitutive of orthodoxy. This insight is a result of his contact with the works of Habermas (Schillebeeckx 1975b: 105). The uncovering of ideology within scripture and its use is an insight from critical theory. Thus, different disciplines helped Schillebeeckx to correct previous misapprehensions about his faith.

In summary, the relationship between theology and other disciplines in Schillebeeckx's method is correlative, that is, they exert a critical influence on each other. This relationship is parallel to Schillebeeckx's method of critical correlation between situation and tradition.

For Frei, on the other hand, the relationship between theology and other disciplines is an ad hoc one — that is, only when there is a need will theology use other disciplines.[7] In his book *Types of Christian Theology*, Frei is interested specifically in the relationship of theology to philosophy, since historically this relationship was the predominant one.

Frei is very much opposed to the extreme situation where "philosophy may be regarded as being a foundational discipline which, rather than giving us information, provides us with the criteria of meaning and certainty, coherence as well as truth, in any arena of human reflection. In other words, the rules of correct thought are invariant and all-fields-encompassing. In the light of its foundational status, philosophy arbitrates what may at any time and anywhere count as meaningful language, genuine thought, and real knowledge. And theology, given its long but also dubious standing in the academy, is a prime candidate for philosophical scrutiny" (Frei 1992: 20). Theology does not simply borrow from philosophy or use the insights of philosophy. Rather, philosophical criteria have priority over Christian self-description (1992: 28). Some theologians such as Kaufman and Tracy look on theology as an academic discipline that is similar to philosophy and thus, must imitate philosophy. In Frei's opinion, they forget that theology is a Christian self-description and, as a result, is a function of the church.

Frei suggests that the most appropriate way to relate theology to philosophy and thus any other discipline is expounded by Barth, who "insists . . . that Christianity has its own distinctive language, which is not to be interpreted without residue into other ways of thinking and speaking" (Frei 1992: 38). Barth,

---

7 I use the term "ad hoc" slightly differently than Frei. Frei uses it to designate the relationship of theology and philosophy in Schleiermacher's theology, namely, as "ad hoc correlation." For Frei, the relationship between theology and other disciplines is ad hoc but not a correlative. That is, neither the standards nor the norms of philosophy apply to theological method (1992: 70).

according to Frei, recognizes theology as Christian self-description which has priority over theology as an academic discipline in two distinct ways. "First, theology is not philosophically founded, and, second, what makes theology an orderly and systematic procedure . . . is for Barth not a set of universal, formal criteria which are certain and all-fields-encompassing. . . . But in addition, . . . theology has its own rules of what makes it a science — a set of rules that are usually implicit and developed only as the context of theology itself develops" (1992: 38-39). Thus, because theology is a self-critical and self-descriptive enterprise, it follows that it is function of the church first and foremost and not simply an academic discipline. "Barth tells us that theology is a function of the Church; specifically, it arises because the Church is accountable to God for its discourse about God. . . . Barth says that the criterion of Christian discourse is the being of the Church, and the being of the Church for him is Jesus Christ, God in his presence or turning to humanity" (1992: 39).

This particular way of relating theology to philosophy is believed to preserve Christian identity in its theological discourse. Christian theological discourse as a self-descriptive and critical activity has its own criteria and rules. How does this relationship between theology and the other disciplines take shape in actual Christian self-description?

In his book *The Identity of Jesus Christ*, Frei makes ad hoc use of non-theological disciplines. He uses the categories of literary theory of Erich Auerbach and the anthropological categories of Gilbert Ryle, for example, to expound and clarify his christology. To understand who and what Jesus is, Frei makes use of Ryle's categories of intention-action and self-manifestation: who and what person is is his or her actions. However, the only place to find Jesus' actions is in the biblical narrative. Frei uses categories from literary theory to identify those actions of Jesus that will manifest his person. "Realistic narrative" becomes the category that is most helpful. It is the unfolding of the story through the way in which the characters interact with each other and their situations. Frei makes use of the two disciplines, literary theory and anthropology, to redescribe Jesus Christ. However, when these categories are no longer useful—which is the case when speaking of the unity of identity and presence and the instance of the resurrection narrative—he discards them and returns to the categories of faith. The move is a theological move. He is not bound by the literary or philosophical categories. His criteria are strictly theological. The literary and philosophical categories are not used to make the Christian message reasonable or intelligible; they only describe it.

In summary, the method that Schillebeeckx uses to answer his question is that of seeking what is common or universal. His method is experientially based because of this anthropological concern. Frei, on the other hand, seeks the different and the specific; he concentrates on Christian faith and what makes it unique. What makes Christianity unique is Jesus Christ. The anthropological aspect is virtually eliminated. Thus, the theological enterprise for Schillebeeckx can be called apologetic, while for Frei it can be called confessional. As to the relationship of theology to other disciplines, Schillebeeckx's approach can be called correlative while Frei's can be called ad hoc.

8

BIBLICAL INTERPRETATION AND
JESUS THE CHRIST

8.1 Biblical Interpretation

In the previous chapter, I outlined the differences between Schillebeeckx and Frei on issues of doctrine and their respective understanding of theology and theological method. My claim was that the use of a certain theological method was not only based on their theological perspectives but also directed by their questions. I will now compare and contrast their ways of interpreting the biblical narrative. For their theological methods become most manifest in their respective styles of biblical interpretation. What both authors believe theology to be, and how it relates to other disciplines, become most clear in the way they read the biblical text.

Their different understandings of revelation are reflected in the way the two authors approach the biblical text. Because for Schillebeeckx revelation is mediated in human experience, the Bible is seen as the document that gives access to the revelation of God through the experience of the disciples and the early church. Thus, the Bible forms the constitution or "charter" for Christians. In his words, "as the Church's 'charter' or foundation document, there can be no substitute for the New Testament's authority" (Schillebeeckx 1979: 59).

In this way, the Bible offers an interpretive framework for subsequent experiences of revelation. If the Bible is seen as the original document of revelation through the experience of the disciples and Jesus, then it follows that in interpreting the Bible it is the experience of the disciples and Jesus that is sought.

However, the experience of the disciples and Jesus witnesses to the reality of God. In other words, the interpreter of the biblical text is interested in the reality to which the biblical text is witness in and through the experience of the disciples and Jesus. "Taking the texts themselves as his point of departure, the interpreter therefore goes beyond the texts and their meaning and inquires about the reality to which the texts intentionally or unintentionally bear witness" (Schillebeeckx 1977: 33). The biblical text bears witness to the grace of God, experienced by Jesus Christ, the disciples and the early church. Methods such as the historical-critical method, literary-critical theories and a host of other methods are some of the tools that are used to uncover that experience.

In the previous chapter, it was established that Schillebeeckx uses those different critical methods to assist him in interpreting the biblical message. The way in which Schillebeeckx uses different methods of biblical interpretation is governed by his understanding of the structure of experience (Schillebeeckx 1980b: 49). He usually starts with an analysis of language. He works with literary-critical methods to arrive at some understanding of what certain words and expressions meant, how they were used in the Hebrew Scriptures and how the New Testament writers also used them. Then he uses historical-critical methods to ascertain the historical situation of the community that gave rise to the particular writing, whether the community's specific historical situation or the wider historical situation. Then he ascertains the writing's theological and philosophical background in an attempt to arrive at the different interpretive frameworks that were constitutive of the community's experience. All this is a means of to understanding how these disciples or the early community experienced and articulated their encounter with God.

As was mentioned earlier, the above is only one element of biblical interpretation. There is also the need for analysis of the present situation in light of which the first element can make sense. Schillebeeckx writes: "What we are concerned with is rather a mutually critical correlation in which we attune our belief and action within the world in which we live, here and now, to what is expressed in the Biblical tradition. This correlation therefore requires: 1. an analysis of our present world or even worlds of experience; 2. an analysis of the constant structures of the fundamental Christian experience about which the New Testament and the rest of the Christian tradition of experience speak, and 3. the critical correlation and on occasion the critical confrontation of these two 'sources'" (Schillebeeckx 1981b: 50-51). An important aspect of Schillebeeckx's method is a careful analysis of our present situation, especially experiences of suffering, of wars, of poverty—that is, experiences of meaninglessness.

In summary, Schillebeeckx's method of biblical interpretation is a method that attempts to arrive at the experience of Jesus, the disciples and the early church, in terms not so much of knowing their experience, but rather of discovering how they witnessed to the reality of God.

Frei, on the other hand, believes that revelation is identical with Jesus Christ and that the Bible is a witness to Jesus Christ. As a result, the Bible has similar characteristics to revelation, as I mentioned in chapter one. If revelation is objective, is about Jesus Christ, is unmediated in human categories and reflects the freedom of God, so must the Bible, or more precisely the meaning of the Bible, be. Thus, in interpreting the Bible what Frei seeks, in contrast to Schillebeeckx, is not the experience of the disciples, Jesus or the early church, to which the Bible is a witness; rather he seeks a meaning that is objective, christocentric, and unmediated, and that reflects the freedom of God.

Frei is most interested in the narrative aspect of the Bible, the biblical narratives, in contrast to Schillebeeckx, who is interested in all its genres. Frei's choice colours his whole outlook. There are several comments that can be made about Frei's understanding of the Bible. The Bible is to be understood as a realistic narrative whose meaning is its literal sense. As a result, it must be interpreted figuratively; its reference is the mystery of Jesus Christ, whose truth cannot be adjudicated by human methods since it is grounded by God. Finally, to understand the biblical narrative is to be able to use it in a fashion similar to the way one understands language by being fluent in it. These characteristics of the biblical narrative have been considered in greater detail in chapter two.

Schillebeeckx takes the route Frei is opposing. The difference between the two theologians is the location of meaning. Frei locates meaning in the story; it is about Jesus Christ since he is the revelation of God. Schillebeeckx locates meaning wherever there are human beings, since that is where revelation is to be found. Thus, for Schillebeeckx meaning is located not only in the text, as Frei holds, but behind the text in the experience of those the story describes, and also in front of the text in the experience of those who read and hear the text communally and personally. Meaning results from what Gadamer calls a "fusion of horizons" (1975: 273), from the constant movement of and critical correlation between situation and tradition. Meaning is neither behind the text alone, nor in front of the text alone nor *in* the text, for that matter. Meaning is in the meeting in a critical fashion of all these elements, with the criteria of meaning coming from the textual and linguistic analysis.

Despite real differences, Schillebeeckx and Frei are not diametrically opposed to each other. Both realize the importance and power of the biblical narrative to shape our lives and our response. However, they move differently towards the goal, which is that one reads the story and identifies with it by making its world one's own on both the communal and the personal levels.

Schillebeeckx claims that "there can be a premature resort to the telling of stories (and so it can provide cover for a lot of injustice, lovelessness and real problems)" (1979: 79). He is referring to first innocence, that is, narrative innocence. In first innocence the story is taken literally. Its depictions are taken as historical facts, and the most illusive danger is to actually imitate every last detail. An example of how one can imitate the scriptural story is to ban women from speaking in the assembly of worshippers, or to continue to believe in slavery as an institution that could be seen as blessed by Paul. That, however, is not what Schillebeeckx (or Frei for that matter) is after. Schillebeeckx is after what he calls "second innocence" (ibid.). In "second innocence" one reads the narrative and identifies with its characters and its world without being naive. This is what I will call a "critical identification," where one identifies not so much with the letter but rather with the spirit of the text. Edith Wyschogrod uses the image of rewriting while reading the narrative: "[The] text lays hold of the reader so that the hermeneutics of reading . . . is transformed into a struggle of writing. That is to say, the addressee must reinscribe, not merely represent, the narrative as her/his own story. In the process of reinscription, a new life is shaped" (1990: 149). In other words, in reading the narrative one rewrites one's life. One does not simply imitate. In rewriting the narrative in one's own life, one already has taken a critical stance towards the narrative. Nevertheless, the distance between text and reader is no longer there. Wyschogrod gives the example of Catherine of Sienna's reading of the passion in the biblical narrative: "It does not help to say Saint Catherine *saw* the passion, although visions of the passion are common. Instead truer to her account, she entered into the passion, felt it with her whole being. Nothing intervened between herself and it. The lack of distance that informs her encounter is experienced as pain" (1990: 16). How does one arrive at the state of "second innocence," of "reinscribing the narrative"? Schillebeeckx gives an answer. "The linguists who argue for rehabilitating the narrative 'innocence,' as I see it, mistakenly fail to appreciate that in a post-critical period man cannot possibly relapse into an 'initial state of primitiveness' (Kierkegaard). So it has to be a 'second innocence,' that is, a style of narration that has been through the 'value free' neutralizing process of the sciences and the interiorizing of consciousness (reflection)" (1979: 79). To arrive at "second innocence," one must go through the muddy waters of pulling the text apart, using, as it were, very disruptive tools such as historical-critical and literary-critical methods. There is no other route to "second innocence" but through the ambiguous and shady space of critical analysis. "When all its analyses and interpretations, reason is no longer able theoretically to express in words what in fact there is still to be said, it is obliged to utter its elusive 'surplus-vested-in-reality' in stories and parables" (ibid.).

The danger, of course, is assuming that critical analysis is the goal of the process. As a result, more theories are constructed and more structures are made to arrive, as it were, at meaning. According to Frei, method takes over and assumes a life of its own, which in turn overwhelms the narrative and its characters, notably Jesus Christ. Method becomes the source of meaning. On this issue, I think Schillebeeckx is in agreement.

In summary, at least on the issue of biblical interpretation there is agreement between the two theologians on the goal, even though they differ concerning the method used to arrive at that goal. Schillebeeckx examines the experience of the disciples, Jesus and the early church on the one hand and ours on the other, not purely as exercises in themselves but rather as a way through which we can "reinscribe" the narrative in our lives to achieve "second innocence." This way of reading the narrative is reminiscent of the way Frei would like us to read the narrative — where we are attentive to the characters and where the distance between us and the text is reduced.[1] In other words, it is the way a community uses the text without assuming that meaning is in the method.

We may conclude by noting that their respective traditions, Catholic and Protestant, have helped shape the understanding of revelation and biblical interpretation of both these theologians. Frei, coming from a Reformed tradition, believes in the priority of the biblical narrative. This Protestant emphasis was an attempt to correct the Catholic dependence on "tradition" that was almost independent of the Bible. One can therefore understand Frei's concern in his earlier writings with biblical meaning as textually based. On the other hand, one can see the logic of Schillebeeckx's interest in experience. True to his Thomistic origins, he sees the created order as where God speaks. Thus, his biblical interpretation seeks that very reality, namely, the experience to which, in his opinion, the biblical narrative is a witness.

Nevertheless, both authors move away from their respective traditions towards each other. By this I mean that in his biblical

---

1 Frei, however, specifically critiques "second innocence" on the grounds that it belongs to the general theory of hermeneutics;, furthermore, it undermines the realistic character of the biblical narrative. See *Theology and Narrative*, 130-40.

interpretation Frei moves towards a Catholic position, while in his Schillebeeckx moves towards a Protestant position. In his later writings, Frei sees the literal meaning of the Bible as communally based; meaning lies in the way the Christian community uses the Bible — traditionally a Catholic position. Schillebeeckx, on the other hand, moves away from his Catholic "tradition" by starting from the biblical narrative, while nevertheless retaining the Catholic interest in human involvement in the form of experience.

8.2 Jesus the Christ

We now turn to the christologies of Schillebeeckx and Frei in relation to their different understandings of revelation and experience.

8.2.1 The Person of Jesus Christ

Frei's understanding of the person of Jesus Christ is based on identity rather than presence. To focus on the question of identity, according to Frei, is to understand the person of Jesus as who or what he is in himself rather than in his relationship to us. Frei does not start from dogmatic affirmations about Jesus Christ, such as the Chalcedonian formula, for two connected reasons. The first reason is related to the way in which he reads the biblical narrative: the biblical narrative does not define Jesus in terms of dogmatic affirmations. The second reason is Frei's fear that to start from a definition such as the Chalcedonian formula is another way of going behind the actions of Jesus and seeking the ghost-in-the-machine and, furthermore, claiming that the ghost is divine. Thus, Frei's christology can be called a "low" christology.[2] It is important to note, however, that Frei's christology is "low," not so much because he is more interested in the humanity of Jesus or roots his christology in experience, but rather because of the way he understands and expands upon Jesus' identity. The categories of literary analysis demand that he

---

2 George Hunsinger (1992: 116-17) claims that Frei's christology is a "low" christology. Frei is reluctant to answer the question of the divinity of Jesus Christ and he skirts the edge of Nestorianism and adoptionism.

look strictly at the biblical narrative, while the categories of anthropology demand that he look strictly at Jesus' action as that which defines his identity.

Schillebeeckx's christology is also seen as a "low" christology.[3] In contrast to Frei's option for understanding Jesus in terms of identity, in which emphasis is laid on Jesus-in-himself, Schillebeeckx opts for understanding Jesus in terms of his relationship to others, whether the disciples, the early church or us. Schillebeeckx, that is, starts with the notion of Jesus' presence.

How, then, is the relationship of Jesus Christ to God to be conceived? For Schillebeeckx, Jesus' person is grounded in his intimate relationship with God which is manifested in his *Abba* experience. The *Abba* experience is also Jesus' experience of contrast. In Schillebeeckx's words, "on the one hand the incorrigible, irremediable history of man's suffering, a history of calamity, violence and injustice, of grinding, excruciating and oppressive enslavement; on the other hand Jesus' particular religious awareness of God, his *Abba* experience, his intercourse with God as the benevolent, solicitous 'one who is against evil,' who will not admit the supremacy of evil and refuses to allow it the last word" (1979: 267). Jesus' *Abba* experience not only relates him to God in a very intimate manner but also relates him with the same intimacy to humanity through the experience of suffering. Thus, Jesus becomes, in Schillebeeckx's favourite words, 'the parable of God and the paradigm of humanity' (1979: 626). For Schillebeeckx, it is Jesus' humanity and the experience of that humanity in the form of suffering that are the basis for his intimate relationship to God and to the human race.

Frei, on the other hand, describes Jesus' identity in terms of intention-action and self-manifestation descriptive categories. He seeks to identify Jesus by a characteristic that unifies his identity. This characteristic is obedience to God. According to Frei, "In the New Testament story, Jesus is seen to enact the good of men on their behalf — or their salvation — in perfect obedience to God. It is not, as we have said, that love to men was his only

---

3 Reginald Fuller (1984: 105-16) claims that Schillebeeckx is not expounding a christology but rather a "Jesusology," i.e., a theology about Jesus, in which titles such as "Son of God" refer to divine commissioning rather than divine ontology.

or even his predominant behavioral quality. Rather, he was perfectly obedient" (1967: 102-103). Out of this relationship of total obedience to God flows Jesus' love for humanity. In other words, Jesus' relationship to God defines his relationship to others. His obedience grounds his actions of love for others. "His obedience to God was one with his intention to do what had to be done on men's behalf. In this way, his mission was identical with love for men" (1967: 103). What defines Jesus' relationship to God is this characteristic of obedience. What defines Jesus' relationship to us is love that is grounded in his relationship to God.

Clearly, then, both theologians draw on their respective anthropologies in order to understand who Jesus is: Schillebeeckx is experientially oriented, giving priority to negative contrast experience, while Frei uses the anthropology of Gilbert Ryle and the category of multi-track dispositions or characteristics.

8.2.2 The Life, Death and Resurrection of Jesus

8.2.2.1 Jesus' Life

How is Jesus' life to be understood, and how is Jesus' person related to his life?

Frei looks on the life of Jesus as that which constitutes the story or the biblical narrative. The characters and circumstances help reveal the unsubstitutable character of Jesus Christ. The story unfolds in three stages. In the first stage of the story, Jesus' birth and infancy narrative, Jesus is a symbol of Israel (Frei 1993: 77). In the second stage of the story, Jesus' baptism and miracles, Jesus' works are symbols of the Kingdom of God (1993: 78). The complete revealing of Jesus' unsubstitutable character occurs in the third stage of the story. Thus, for Frei, the life of Jesus is the unfolding of his story as he becomes his unsubstitutable self. It is interesting to note that, although Frei's whole project is to locate the meaning of the narrative in the story itself rather than in ostensive reference to ideas, historical facts or even symbolically to our lives, in his analysis of the first two stages of Jesus' life Frei interprets them symbolically rather than simply in reference to Jesus.

For Schillebeeckx, the life of Jesus is central. It is in light of Jesus' life that both Jesus' death and his resurrection have meaning. Moreover, it is Jesus' life that gives meaning to salvation and it is Jesus' life that defines what he meant by the Kingdom of God. "[T]he kingdom of God has to be defined further in terms of the life of Jesus: in terms of the fact that where sick people came to Jesus they were healed; in terms of the encounter of 'demonic spirits of sickness' which become whole in their encounter with Jesus; in terms of his table fellowship and dealings with 'tax collectors and sinners' who in his time were those who were marginalized, discriminated against and even excommunicated; in terms of his beatitudes on the poor; and finally in terms of all the oppressed" (Schillebeeckx 1990: 112). Even God "can be 'defined' only from and in terms of the human career of Jesus" (1990: 121). Thus, for Schillebeeckx, Jesus' career is the basis of everything we say about Jesus, even affirming him as the Christ. In Schillebeeckx's words, "it was this message and these actions, the whole historical phenomenon of Jesus, which led certain people to recognize in him 'the Christ' — decisive salvation from God — in an act of faith. . . . Jesus was not proclaimed to be the Christ despite or apart from what he really was in history" (1981b: 28-29).

8.2.2.2 Jesus' Death on the Cross

Both authors differ on this issue also. Frei believes that, as the story moves towards the cross, Jesus becomes more and more himself, no longer the symbol of Israel or the Kingdom of God. Frei writes: "In terms of the movement that we have traced, from a symbolic or representative person to an individual in his own right, we have reached the last stage of the story. There is no further focusing of his identity. In this respect, the passion and resurrection represent, in the very transition from one to the other, not two stages, but one. In both, he is equally himself, none other than Jesus of Nazareth. In the unity of this particular transition, passion and resurrection, he is most of all himself, most historical as an individual in his own right " (1993: 80). Furthermore, Jesus' death on the cross, for Frei, is seen as the manifestation of his unifying characteristic, namely, obedience. He was obedient to God even unto the cross. Finally, the death of Jesus cannot be separated from the resurrection, for in both Jesus is his unsubstitutable self. And in both is the salvation of humanity.

Schillebeeckx has a radically different perspective on the death of Jesus. First, he sees it as a symbol of evil which cannot be explained away, and cannot be spiritualized, that is, given meaning, without being made into a tool for further oppression. Evil is a mystery that cannot be rationalized. In his words, "[T]he cross was . . . the sealing of the superior power of human beings over God. . . . In that case suffering and death remain absurd, and even in Jesus' case may not be mystified" (Schillebeeckx 1990: 128). We cannot even say that we are saved by it. In a stark sentence, Schillebeeckx claims that "we have to say that we are not redeemed *thanks* to the death of Jesus but *despite* it" (Schillebeeckx 1980b: 729). For Schillebeeckx, the death of Jesus has no meaning in and of itself; its meaning emerges only in light of his life. Jesus' death is the consequence of a life in service of justice and love, a consequence of his option for the poor and outcast. In other words, "Jesus' whole life is the hermeneusis of his death" (1979: 311).

Schillebeeckx, then, sees the violent death of Jesus on the cross as a symbol of evil that has no meaning in itself, that cannot be mystified, or explained away. Like any other evil, it has no efficacy. It has meaning only in light of Jesus' life which was lived for others in spite of the looming danger. For Frei, on the other hand, the death of Jesus on the cross is necessary for the resurrection, through which Jesus emerges as himself and through which we are saved.

8.2.2.3 The Resurrection

For Frei, as mentioned above, the death of Jesus on the cross and the resurrection are inseparable. It is in this third stage of the story of Jesus that he emerges as his own self. His unsubstitutable and singular identity emerges then, since in the resurrection Jesus' identity and presence are made one. "He emerged fully as the one unsubstitutable Jesus of Nazareth — and this as much in the resurrection as in the passion" (Frei 1967: 136). For Frei, it is in the resurrection that the activity of God is manifested. Frei writes: "In his passion and death the initiative of Jesus disappears more and more into that of God; but in the resurrection, where the initiative of God is finally and decisively climaxed and he alone is and can be active, the sole identity to mark the presence of that activity is Jesus. God remains hidden, and even reference to him is almost altogether lacking. Jesus of Nazareth, he and none other, marks the presence of the action of God" (1967: 121). Frei, as we can see, looks at the resurrection from two vantage points. The first is that of the unfolding of the story of Jesus: in the passion and resurrection Jesus becomes himself. From the second, theological, vantage point, it is in the resurrection that God's activity and human activity become one and the hidden God becomes manifest. The resurrection is seen totally in terms of Jesus and God; that is, although it is efficacious in that it results in the saving of humanity, the resurrection itself is something strictly between God and Jesus. This is in contrast to Schillebeeckx's approach.

For Schillebeeckx, the resurrection, like the death of Jesus, cannot be understood except in light of Jesus' life. Schillebeeckx claims that the New Testament offers us no account of the resurrection considered in and of itself; all we have is the account of some of Jesus' followers who at the hour of his crucifixion scattered and were filled with fear, but who at a later time started a movement even in the face of death. Thus, "anyone who has at first taken offence at Jesus and subsequently proclaims him to be the only bringer of salvation has of necessity undergone a 'conversion process.' As a first reply to the question: What actually took place between the two historical events — Jesus' death and the apostles' preaching — we are therefore bound to say at once: the conversion of the disciples" (Schillebeeckx 1979: 381). Schillebeeckx proposes that it is in the conversion experience of the disciples from fear to fearlessness that belief in the resurrection emerges.[4] Because of their experience of the abiding pres-

---

4 Some theologians disagree with Schillebeeckx on his interpretation of the resurrection and believe that he has reduced the resurrection merely to a subjective experience. See Fackre 1984: 248-77; Haughey 1981: 201-207; and Scheffczyk 1984: 383-408.

ence of Jesus Christ, the disciples concluded that Jesus must have been raised from the dead. But they could have reached this conclusion only on the basis of their experience of Jesus while he was alive. "Thus we end up in a remarkable hermeneutical circle: Jesus' living and dying on earth suggested to Christians, in virtue of their experiences after Jesus' death, the idea of the resurrection or of the coming Parousia of Jesus, while on the basis of their faith in the risen or coming crucified One they relate the story of Jesus in the gospels" (1979: 401).

The differing approaches of Schillebeeckx and Frei to the issue of the resurrection reflect their different evaluations of the place and importance of human experience in theology and faith. Frei views the resurrection as an event that is solely between Jesus and God and that is hidden from us. Jesus was obedient to God and God vindicated Jesus by raising him up. The resurrection, a miracle and an event (Frei 1993: 203), is seen strictly as an objective happening. In Frei's opinion, the resurrection is real and "historical," but not similar to other historical events that can be verified by historical methods, because it is a singular event. Schillebeeckx, on the other hand, regards the resurrection as the way the disciples articulated the experience of conversion in light of their experience of the life and abiding presence of Jesus. It is in light of Jesus' life that they adopted the resurrection as a model to explain what they had experienced.

8.2.3 *The Salvific Work of Jesus*

Finally, Schillebeeckx and Frei have differing soteriologies. Frei believes that Jesus' death and resurrection save us for two connected reasons, both derived from the patristic principle that is made of two parts: first, that Jesus was fully human; second, that we are all included in Jesus' humanity. The patristic principle assumes a continuity between Jesus of Nazareth and the resurrected Christ. "The point of the stories is simply to bear witness to the fact that Jesus, raised from the dead, was the same person, the same identity as before. That is the central Christian affirmation, vigorously reaffirmed both in the Creeds and in this article with its stress on the physical nature of the risen Jesus—a physicality that is indispensable if he is to be efficacious on our behalf. The great Patristic saying, 'What he did not assume [i.e., anything less than full humanity], that he could not save' is as true of him in the resurrection as in his life before death" (Frei 1993: 204). The patristic principle requires not only that the identity of Jesus be continuous before and after death, but also that we be included in the humanity of Jesus. "Even more startling than the continuity of the identity of Jesus through death and resurrection is the affirmation associated with it in Christian faith: his identity as this singular, continuing individual Jesus of Nazareth includes humankind in its singularity. He is the representative and inclusive person. That, together with his efficacy to save, is what the New Testament tells us about him: the Word of God is the man whose very identity it is to be for others, and as this single individual to live, die, and be raised on their behalf" (Frei 1993: 204-205). Jesus saves us by his death and resurrection. However, just as Frei's christology is objective, so is his soteriology. In Hunsinger's words, "Frei's narrative christology, as focused on the pattern of exchange, commits him to what might be called an objectivist soteriology. Salvation, that is to say, is defined primarily as what takes place vicariously in the life, death and resurrection of Christ. The story in which Jesus enacts his identity and the story of our salvation are not two different stories. The story of salvation is the story he enacts — the story of his obedience in redeeming guilty men by vicarious identification with their guilt and literal identification with their helplessness" (1993: 252). In other words, Jesus saves through his life, death and resurrection irrespective of acceptance or rejection by the recipient of salvation. Frei does not expand on the subjective aspect of salvation, for the same reason that he does not start with the presence of Jesus. If to understand salvation one started with the subjective pole, one might never arrive at the issue of the work of Jesus, but would be lost in the conditions of salvation's reception by us. Frei has a christocentric soteriology; that is, it is Jesus Christ who saves. Although Frei has a "low" christology, delineated by his literal reading of the narrative, he has a "high" depiction of his work (Hunsinger 1993: 250).

Schillebeeckx has a different understanding of the work of Jesus. The whole project of Schillebeeckx in his books on Jesus is an attempt to understand salvation. Salvation, for Schillebeeckx, is the continuing activity of God in and through Jesus Christ, which is further mediated in and through the praxis of those who are working to counter evil in the world.

Claims about the saving activity of God in and through Jesus can only be seen, in Schillebeeckx's opinion, in terms of the continuation of the saving activity of God experienced during the earthly life of Jesus. Thus, "Jesus' caring and abiding presence among people" (Schillebeeckx 1979: 179), manifested in miracles, his freedom to do good, his table fellowship which excluded no one and his invitation to others to have faith in God (1979: 180-200), was experienced as liberating and joyous (1979: 200) and thus revealed "the 'beneficent' reality of God's lordship" (1979: 179). In other words, salvation is not simply the result of the death of Jesus, for the life of Jesus is the source that made his death a "saving" death. In Schillebeeckx's words, "it can hardly be said that to accord with Jesus' self-understanding his message of salvation took its meaning only from his death. The truth is: he died just as he lived, and he lived as he died" (1979: 306).

A second important difference between Schillebeeckx and Frei is that salvation for Schillebeeckx is enacted by God, while for Frei it is Jesus who saves. In other words, Schillebeeckx's soteriology is theocentric while that of Frei is christocentric. Schillebeeckx's soteriology is evident from a phrase he often uses: "salvation in Jesus from God" (Schillebeeckx 1980b: 194; 292; 631); it is God who saves in and through Jesus Christ.

Finally, Schillebeeckx and Frei differ on the question of the mediation of salvation. For Schillebeeckx, as humans are co-creators with God so are they the mediators of God's salvation in their actions to counter evil. Through their liberating praxis, they give glimpses, however fragmentary, of God's final salvation. Schillebeeckx gives a summary of what he means by salvation: "What, then, is salvation in Jesus from God? I would want to say: being at the disposal of others, losing oneself to others (each in his own limited situation) and within this 'conversion' (which is also made possible by structural changes) also working through anonymous structures for the happiness, the goodness and the truth of mankind. This way of life, born of grace, provides a real possibility for a very personal encounter with God, who is then experienced as the source of all happiness and salvation, the source of joy" (1980b: 838). Frei, on the other hand, does not mention the issue of mediation of salvation by other humans. Salvation is strictly through the death and resurrection of Jesus Christ.

In summary, for Frei salvation is in and through the death and resurrection of Jesus Christ. Frei's soteriology is objectivist. This is in contrast to Schillebeeckx, who believes that the praxis of liberation of others mediates God's saving activity, both in Jesus and in us.

8.3 Conclusion

In the last three chapters, I have compared Schillebeeckx and Frei, contending that their understanding of revelation and its mediation in history affects the way they view the role of experience in theological method, which in turn affects their resulting theology, in this case christology.

I first compared these theologians' understanding of revelation: Schillebeeckx stresses the mediated character of revelation, while Frei stresses the simple fact that Jesus Christ came. Their differing understanding of revelation is bound up with the fundamental questions that they attempt to answer. Schillebeeckx is primarily concerned with hermeneutical questions, not only on the intellectual level but also on the level of praxis. Frei, on the other hand, is concerned first with the identity of Jesus Christ and then (in his later work) with the identity of the Christian community. Because of the nature of their understanding of revelation and the nature of their questions, their methods diverge. Schillebeeckx seeks a common anthropological and experiential starting point, which, because of his concern with the question of suffering, is the negative contrast experience. Frei, on the other hand, focuses on questions of identity, and seeks what is partic-

ular, that which sets Christ and Christians apart. In his earlier
work, the particular is the identity of Jesus Christ; in his later
work, this is supplemented by an interest in the particular identity of the Christian community. From this methodology
emerges the different ways in which these theologians interpret
the Bible. Schillebeeckx's interest is in the reality to which the
Bible witnesses—namely, the experience of salvation from God
in Jesus Christ—in an attempt to explore the possibility of the
contemporary experience of that same salvation from God
through Jesus. Schillebeeckx employs several methods in his
search for that reality: he uses literary-critical and historical-critical methods to arrive at a better understanding of what it means
to be saved by God in Jesus; he goes behind, in front and on the
surface of the text to arrive at such an understanding. Frei, on the
other hand, in seeking the identity of Jesus Christ, seeks only the
particular. Thus, Frei concentrates only on the surface of the
text—namely, the story about Jesus Christ—since that is where
revelation took place.

This brought us to the two theologians' christology. Frei's
christology could be seen as objective, interested in Jesus in himself. Although one might expect Frei to propose a "high" christology, with considerable attention paid to the divinity of Jesus,
that is not the case. This may be because an "ontological" "high"
christology could be seen as seeking an ascriptive subject behind
the actions instead of simply looking at the actions—that is, as
seeking the "ghost-in-the-machine." Furthermore, it would
mean that one reads into the biblical narrative later historical
developments such as the christological dogma of the Council of
Chalcedon. In that sense, although Frei's is a christology that is
interested in Jesus in himself, it is not a "high" christology but,
rather a "low" christology. However, this does not mean that it
starts with human experience, but rather that it starts from the
given text. Schillebeeckx's christology is seen as a "low" christology since it starts from the experience of the disciples and
Jesus. However, Schillebeeckx, like Frei, does not make the leap
to the Chalcedonian formula, because he understands the titles
of Jesus, such as "Son of God" and "Christ," not as reflecting

ontological realities about Jesus, but rather as reflecting the complex reality of the disciples' experience of him. Schillebeeckx's christology could be labelled relational, while that of Frei is objective; both are "low" christologies.

9

EXPERIENCE AND THEOLOGY

The complexity of questions about the use of experience as a source for theology cannot be reduced to a simple dichotomy, whereby either one opts for a particular theological method that uses experience as one of its aspects or one simply opts for another method that does not use experience at all. Even those who agree in general on the use of experience in theological method disagree about how it should be used and whose experience is to be used. And those who dispute that experience is a source of theology do so not simply on methodological grounds, but also on theological grounds.

9.1 The Issue of Experience: Convergence or Divergence?

In the previous chapter, I summarized the different approaches of Frei and Schillebeeckx. In what follows, I will explore the points of similarity between them, using a typology developed by Schner (1992a: 40-59) which maps out the different ways in which theologians have appealed to experience: the appeal transcendental; the appeal hermeneutical; the appeal constructive; the appeal confessional; and, finally, the appeal immediate or mystical.

The appeal transcendental, according to Schner, is the appeal that sees experience as the condition of the possibility of being human. Experience is seen more as a universal category that establishes the condition of possibility rather than a concrete reality with a certain content. In his words, "when experience enters a theological argument in the form of an appeal to an anthropology, it functions as an extreme of the objectification of experience. . . . The appeal is not to any actual descriptions of experience, but to the 'condition of possibility' of all experience, of the structuring elements which make experience human" (Schner 1992a: 52). As to the question of the transcendent, i.e., God, transcendentalists assume that the transcendent is a condition of the possibility of being human, while the life of the community coincides with experience. Theologians such as Rahner and Lonergan fall into this category.

The second appeal to experience is the appeal hermeneutical. According to Schner, this appeal is a critique of the universal, ahistorical appeal transcendental. The appeal hermeneutical emphasizes the historical, conditional and ideological elements within experience. Its stance is one of suspicion. "The appeal hermeneutical questions the very possibility of such an assertion [appeal transcendental] by making explicit in the appeal the perspectival, limited, and even alienating characteristics of experience . . . the appeal hermeneutical emphasizes the dialectical character and function of any appeal" (Schner 1992a: 53). The transcendent is seen as embodied in different forms, while the community is seen in different manifestations, the pluralistic nature of human experience thereby being recognized. Into this category Schner puts what he terms the "perspectival theologians."

The third appeal to experience is the appeal constructive. Here, experience is seen as an interruptive force that catalyzes a transformation. Experience "enters an argument not as foundational but as interruptive. It enters as a moment of discontinuity into a larger, already established context" (Schner 1992a: 54). In contrast to the extremes of the appeals transcendental and hermeneutical, the appeal constructive seems to take the middle line. Experience is neither universal nor relative, yet it retains its normativity and its particularity. Experience "enters into a theological argument without imposing a universal structure independent of the particularities of the religion's community and its beliefs, or without depriving itself of normativity through a presupposed relativity of all experience as mere convention or incommensurate subjectives" (ibid.). Thus, the place and activity of the transcendent are located in the interruptive aspect of experience: it is the "no" that is the agency of God and that is experienced in our lives. Community and tradition have a dual role: they mediate but also hide the transcendent. Into this category Schner puts Barth.

The fourth appeal to experience is the appeal confessional. In Schner's words, it is "an outright appeal to authority, with or without a mention of 'experience'" (1992a: 55). Thus, experience is normative; but here "experience" refers to the life of the church. This appeal to experience "might consist in simply 'telling the story,' recounting the experience, in the hope that the mere hearing of it will inaugurate the moment of transformation and reconstruction" (ibid.). In this appeal there seems to be a close connection between the transcendent and the community. Schner puts homiletic and devotional theologians into this category.

The final appeal to experience is the appeal immediate or mystical. According to Schner, "radical self-transcendence into that which is beyond the self does not admit of mediation, though one might move back into a former mode of appeal and attempt a description of the state of self and its object, with the help of the imagination" (1992a: 57). In this appeal the subject collapses into what is experienced. Thus, there is coincidence of the subject and the transcendent, with very little place for the community.

This schematic outline of the different appeals to experience does not deal in detail with the nuances of the different theologians, especially their theological stance. However, I will use it as a general guideline to identify some overlaps between Schillebeeckx and Frei.

Because Frei is heir to Barth's theological stance on many issues, notably revelation and the place of experience, one would imagine that he would fit the third appeal to experience, namely, the appeal constructive. Experience here is seen as interruptive and transformative, entering the theological argument neither as a universal structure nor simply as a relative structure. Yet, experience retains some normativity even though it is connected with the particularities of the community. The interruptive experience becomes the action of the transcendent: community and tradition are vehicles for the transcendent.

Does Frei fit this category? Since Frei does not speak of experience in his earlier work, and refers to the life of the church as the source of meaning in his later work, one might argue that he does not appeal to experience at all— interruptive, transformative or otherwise. Nevertheless, in his later work, he believes in the normativity of the Christian community's life and language, and this may be construed as an appeal constructive.

What about the fourth appeal to experience, the appeal confessional? The proponents of the appeal confessional turn to authority—for example, by a simple retelling of the story; this could be viewed as a naive understanding of the biblical narrative. In this mode of theology, the transcendent and the community are closely related and both are spoken of in particular terms. In some ways, Frei fits better the appeal confessional. In his earlier work, he believes in the retelling of the story and in its transformative power. His appeal for a single reading of the story without the overwhelming edifice of hermeneutical and historical-critical methods could be seen as a call for a straightforward and even naive reading of the Bible. When Frei emphasizes the church community in his later work, its identity, like that of Jesus Christ, has to be defined in terms of particularities. In that sense, Frei seems to share some of the ideas of the proponents of the appeal confessional. As to the issue of authority, there is some debate. Frei does appeal to authority, but not necessarily a community's authority. For Frei, it is God's authority that grounds truth. In his words, "the text is 'witness' to the Word of God and . . . its authority derives from that witness rather than from any inherent divinized quality. And is that Word which is witnessed to, is that not the truth, at once ontologically transcendent and historically incarnate?" (1993: 163). However, the meaning of the biblical narrative is defined by the community's use. Thus, the literal sense of the Bible is "rooted . . . in its primary and original context, a religious community's 'rule' for faithful reading" (1993: 139). Frei does not equate the transcendent with the community as the proponents of the appeal confessional do. Thus, Frei overlaps with the proponents of the appeal confessional without coinciding altogether with them. Frei does not seem to fit neatly into one category or the other, yet his insights overlap with those theologians who appeal to experience as an appeal constructive and with those theologians who appeal to experience as an appeal confessional.

Schillebeeckx is even more complex. At first glance, one could say that he fits the appeal hermeneutical. On a closer look, however, that judgment does not seem to hold, in that Schillebeeckx is influenced by critical theory and therefore builds an element of suspicion into his theology. But this element of suspicion does not have the final word, for trust in God is greater than any ideology.

Schillebeeckx is best seen as combining the appeal transcendental, the appeal hermeneutical, the appeal constructive and the appeal confessional. He has insights that are common to all four. In his understanding of the priority of grace and God's love, he shares with proponents of the appeal transcendental a theological anthropology that sees God as prior to and necessary for the condition of being human. The transcendent is so much a part of the definition and being of the human that it becomes a dimension of human experience or, more precisely, a dimension of the human. That does not mean that the transcendent and the human are equal partners in the relationship. Rather, it is a way to emphasize the priority and absolute importance of God. Schillebeeckx shares with the proponents of the appeal transcendental a belief in the universal and unconditional love of God. Like others who make similar use of experience, Schillebeeckx's appeal to experience is not purely a methodological move, but rather a theological choice.

Schillebeeckx shares with proponents of the appeal hermeneutical two important insights. The first is the suspicion that what people claim to be universal may conceal an agenda that is more likely than not to be for the good of those in power. The second, bound up with his awareness of the historical conditioning of all that we claim to be universal, is an insight into the perspectival nature of our existence, understanding and claims.

Schillebeeckx shares with proponents of the appeal constructive the insight that experience can be interruptive and thus transformative. This insight comes from the critical theorists' belief that theory and praxis are intimately related. For Schillebeeckx, the most interruptive experience is the experience of evil in the world. Experiences of poverty, war, oppression and hunger are revelatory precisely because they are interruptive. From these interruptive experiences of evil arises the imperative to act, to counter evil.

Schillebeeckx shares with proponents of the appeal confessional the insight of the importance of "telling the story." In a way, Schillebeeckx does not believe that critical analysis is the goal of theology, since of itself it does not create meaning. We must utilize critical analysis in order to pass from the first innocence to second innocence, that is, a reading of the story that is not simplistic or simply critical, but a reading that allows the story to empower us. Yet, Schillebeeckx does not support the appeal to authority which is an element of the appeal confessional.

In summary, then, Schillebeeckx spans several categories. His appeal transcendental is rooted in his understanding of grace; his appeal hermeneutical is rooted in his understanding of human historicity; and his appeal constructive is rooted in the insight he has drawn from critical theory concerning the relationship of theory and praxis and the question of evil. Finally, his appeal confessional for Schillebeeckx is rooted in his desire for the second innocence, on the other side of critical analysis.

This typology helps identify similarities between Schillebeeckx and Frei. Schillebeeckx combines insights from the appeals transcendental, hermeneutical, constructive and confessional. Frei, on the other hand, combines insights from the appeal constructive and the appeal confessional. Thus, Schillebeeckx and Frei seem to share insights from the appeal constructive and the appeal confessional. In the appeal constructive they agree that the life of faith is a lived life and not simply a matter of concepts. Their second point of agreement is the importance of the life of the church. In the appeal confessional they also agree on the importance and the power of the biblical story. Both want the biblical story to be read simply. In his earlier work, Frei believes that a simple reading of the biblical narrative can be accomplished by a literal reading, while Schillebeeckx believes that the same goal can be achieved only when critical analysis has been applied to the narrative. Ironically, Schillebeeckx's attempt to go back to the biblical narrative in order to arrive at the root experience is a way of supplementing the traditional "Catholic" concern with meaning in "tradition" with a more traditional "Protestant" concern with the biblical narrative. Frei, on the other hand, moves from a traditionally "Protestant" concern with *sola scriptura* to a more "Catholic" concern with "tradition." Frei and Schillebeeckx do not so much agree as converge at a middle point at which they arrive from different starting points.

9.2 Final Reflections

This book has claimed that the belief one holds about the doctrine of revelation and God's activity will shape one's attitude towards experience. This is not a linear relationship in which one first decides what one believes about revelation and then, as a corollary, decides what one believes about experience. Beliefs about divine action, mediation and revelation act as interpretive frameworks that shape particular convictions about experience.

Convictions about revelation and divine activity shape the answer to questions about whether experience is necessary for theology proper, define in broad terms what constitutes experience and finally affect how experience is used. The attitude towards experience and its use in turn shapes the subsequent theology. There is, in other words, a circular or spiral movement, in which theological beliefs and propositions affect one's understanding and attitude towards experience, i.e., what it is and how it is to be used, a fact that further affects subsequent theological propositions.

In this book, the circular character of the place of experience in theology is illustrated by christology. If one's understanding of revelation is that it is best understood as the activity of God in human history and reality (in more traditional Catholic language, a more grace-centred theology), then human experience in any form is central. This in turn affects how one interprets the reality of Jesus: human reality becomes intrinsic to christological understanding. Christology, becomes more functional, and soteriology is central to it. By contrast, if revelation is understood as christocentric, then the human part of the equation becomes less important. The resulting christology may become more ontological and more removed from human reality. Furthermore, the person of Jesus may become more removed from his works. In this way, one may claim that theological method is inseparable from doctrinal commitment. An argument about method, whether one's own method or one's critique of another's, is always bound up with theological judgments. In theology, method involves the theological agenda of its proponent.

BIBLIOGRAPHY

Adorno, T.
1992   "Why Philosophy." In *Critical Theory: The Essential Readings*,
        ed. D. Ingram and J. Simon-Ingram, 20-30. New York:
        Paragon House.
Ateek, S.
1989   *Justice and Only Justice: A Palestinian Theology of Liberation.*
        Maryknoll: Orbis Books.
Auerbach, E.
1953   *Mimesis: The Presentation of Reality in Western Literature.*
        Trans. W. Trask. Princeton: Princeton University Press.
Barnes, P.
1990   "Relativism, Ineffability, and the Appeal to Experience."
        Modern Theology 7: 101-14.
Barth, Karl
1933   *The Epistle to the Romans.* 2nd ed., trans. E. Hoskyns. London:
        Oxford University Press.
1935   *The Word of God and the Word of Man.* Trans. D. Horton.
        London: Hodder and Stoughton.
1936   *God in Action.* Edinburgh: T. & T. Clark.
1956   *Church Dogmatics.* Vol. IV, Part I, trans. G.W. Bromiley.
        Edinburgh: T. & T. Clark.
1975   *Church Dogmatics.* Vol. I, Part I. Edinburgh: T. & T. Clark.
1986   "Fate and Idea in Theology." In *The Way of Theology in Karl
        Barth*, ed. H.M. Rumscheidt, 25-61. Pennsylvania: Pickwick
        Publications.
Batdorf, I.
1984   "Interpreting Jesus Since Bultmann: Selected Paradigms
        and Their Hermeneutic Matrix." *Society of Biblical Literature:
        Seminar Papers* 23: 187-215.

Baum, G.
1981   "Response to Edward Schillebeeckx." *America* 144 (12): 254-58.
Benhabib, S.
1992   "The Utopian Dimension Is Communicative Ethics." In *Critical Theory: The Essential Readings*, ed. D. Ingram and J. Simon-Ingram, 388-89. New York: Paragon House.
Bernstein, R.
1992   *The New Constellation: The Ethical-Political Horizons of Modernity Postmodernity.* Cambridge: MIT Press.
Bleicher, J.
1980   *Contemporary Hermeneutics: Hermeneutics as Method, Philosophy and Critique.* London: Routledge and Kegan Paul.
Blocher, H.
1989   "Biblical Narrative and Historical Reference." In *Issues of Faith and History*, ed. N. Cameron, 102-22. Edinburgh: Rutherford House.
Boff, C.
1987   *Theology and Praxis: Epistemological Foundations.* Maryknoll: Orbis Books.
Bonino, M.
1975   "Hermeneutics, Truth and Praxis." In *Doing Theology in a Revolutionary Situation*, 86-105. Philadelphia: Fortress Press.
Bots, J.
1979   "Dutch Catholicism in Historical Perspective, 1919-1977." *Communio* 6: 294-320.
Bowden, J.
1983   *Edward Schillebeeckx: In Search of the Kingdom of God.* New York: Crossroad.
Buckley, J.
1990   "The Hermeneutical Deadlock Between Revelationists, Textualists and Functionalists." *Modern Theology* 6: 325-39.
1992   *Seeking the Humanity of God: Practices, Doctrines and Catholic Theology.* Collegeville: Liturgical Press.
Buckley, M.
1987   *At the Origins of Modern Atheism.* New Haven: Yale University Press.
1992   "The Rise of Atheism and the Religious Epoche." *CTSA Proceedings* 47: 69-83.
Bultmann, R.
1934   *Jesus and the Word.* New York: Charles Scribner's Sons.
1951   *Theology of the New Testament*, Vol. 1. New York: Charles Scribner's Sons.
1962   *Kerygma and Myth: A Theological Debate.* Ed. H. W. Bartsch. London: SPCK Press.

1968   *Existence and Faith*. Ed. S. Ogden. New York: Meridian Books.

1969   *Faith and Understanding*. Ed. R. Funk. New York: Harper and Row.

1984   *New Testament and Mythology and Other Basic Writings*. Ed. S. Ogden. Philadelphia: Fortress Press.

Busch, E.

1976   *Karl Barth: His Life from Letters and Autobiographical Texts*. Trans. J. Bowden. London: SCM Press.

Chopp, R.

1987   "Feminism's Theological Pragmatism." *Journal of Religion* 67: 239-56.

Comstock, G.

1986   "Truth and Meaning: Ricoeur Versus Frei on Biblical Narrative." *Journal of Religion* 66 (2): 117-40.

1989   "Everything Depends on the Type of the Concepts that the Interpretation Is Made to Convey." *Modern Theology* 5: 215-37.

Cone, J.

1975   *God of the Oppressed*. San Francisco: Harper and Row.

Croatto, S.

1989   *Biblical Hermeneutics*. New York: Crossroad.

Davis, C.

1973   "Theology and Praxis." *Cross Currents* 23: 154-68.

Demson, D.

1992   "Response to David Lowe." *Modern Theology* 8 (2): 145-48.

Duke, J.

1977   "Reading the Gospel Realistically." *Encounter* 38: 296-306.

Dulles, A.

1979   "Hermeneutical Theory." *Communio* 6: 16-37.

Dupré, L.

1982   "Experience and Interpretation: A Philosophical Reflection on Schillebeeckx's *Jesus* and *Christ*." *Theological Studies* 43: 30-51.

Ellingsen, M.

1983   "Luther as Narrative Exegete." *Journal of Religion* 63: 394-413.

Fackre, G.

1984   "Bones Strong and Weak in the Skeletal Structure of Schillebeeckx's Christology." *Journal of Ecumenical Studies* 21 (1): 248-77.

Fiorenza, E.

1984   *Bread not Stone: The Challenge of Feminist Biblical Interpretation*. Boston: Beacon Press.

1989   *In Memory of Her: A Feminist Theological Reconstruction of Christian Origins*. New York: Crossroad.

1992   *But She Said: Feminist Practices of Biblical Interpretation*. Boston: Beacon Press.

Fitzmyer, J.
1986   *Scripture and Christology: A Statement of the Biblical Commission with a Commentary*. New York: Paulist Press.

Ford, D.
1989   "System, Story and Performance." In *Why Narrative?: Readings in Narrative Theology*, ed. S. Hauerwas and L.G. Jones, 191-215. Grand Rapids: Eerdmans Publishing Company.
1992   "Hans Frei and the Future of Theology." *Modern Theology* 8 (2): 203-14.

Frei, Hans
1956   *The Doctrine of Revelation in the Thought of Karl Barth, 1909 to 1922*. Ph.D. diss., Yale University.
1967   *The Identity of Jesus Christ*. Philadelphia: Fortress Press.
1974   *The Eclipse of Biblical Narrative*. New Haven: Yale University Press.
1975   "H. Richard Niebuhr as Christian Theologian." In *Faith and Ethics: The Theology of H. Richard Niebuhr*, ed. P. Ramsey, 2-112. New York: Harper and Brothers.
1987   "Response to 'Narrative Theology: An Evangelical Appraisal.'" *Trinity Journal* 8: 21-24.
1988   "Barth and Schleiermacher: Divergence and Convergence." In *Barth and Schleiermacher: Beyond the Impasse*, ed. J. Duke and R. Streetman, 65-87. Philadelphia: Fortress Press.
1989   "How It All Began: On the Resurrection of Jesus." *Anglican and Episcopal History* 58: 139-45.
1990   "'Narrative' in Christian and Modern Reading." In *Theology and Dialogue: Essays in Conversation with George Lindbeck*, ed. B. Marshall, 149-64. Notre Dame: University of Notre Dame Press.
1991   "H. Richard Niebuhr on History, Church and Nation." In *The Legacy of H. Richard Niebuhr*, ed. R. Thiemann, 1-23. Minneapolis: Fortress Press.
1992   *Types of Christian Theology*. Ed. G. Hunsinger and W. Placher. New Haven: Yale University Press.
1993   *Theology and Narrative: Selected Essays*. Ed. G. Hunsinger and W. Placher. Oxford: Oxford University Press.

Fuller, R.
1984   "Theology of Jesus or Christology?: An Evaluation of the Recent Discussion." *Semeia* 30: 105-16.

Gadamer, H-G.
1975   *Truth and Method*. New York: Seabury Press.

Galvin, J.
  1980   "The Uniqueness of Jesus and His Abba Experience in the Theology of Edward Schillebeeckx." *CTSA Proceedings* 35: 309-14.
  1981   "Schillebeeckx's Retracting the Story of Jesus: Theology as Narrative." *Worldview* 24 (4): 10-12.
Gelpi, D.
  1994   *The Turn to Experience in Contemporary Theology.* New York: Paulist Press.
George, W.
  1985   "The Praxis of the Kingdom of God: Ethics in Schillebeeckx's *Jesus* and *Christ.*" *Horizons* 12: 44-69.
Gerhart, M.
  1989   "The Restoration of Biblical Narrative." *Semeia* 46: 13-23.
Green, Garett, ed.
  1987   *Scriptural Authority and Narrative Interpretation.* (Festschrift for Hans Frei). Philadelphia: Fortress Press.
Green, Geoffrey
  1982   *Literary Criticism and the Structures of History, Erich Auerbach and Leo Spitzer.* Lincoln: University of Nebraska Press.
Gregson, V.
  1985   *Lonergan, Spirituality and the Meeting of Religions.* Lanhamm: University Press of America.
Guarino, T.
  1990   "Revelation and Foundationalism: Toward Hermeneutical and Ontological Appropriateness." *Modern Theology* 6: 221-34.
Gutiérrez, G.
  1971   *A Theology of Liberation: History, Politics, and Salvation.* Maryknoll: Orbis Books.
Habermas, J.
  1990   *Moral Consciousness and Communicative Action.* Cambridge: MIT Press.
Haight, R. and M. Hilkert
  1991   "Liberationist and Feminist Themes in Edward Schillebeeckx's *Church: The Human Story of God.*" *CTSA Proceedings* 46: 114-17.
Hauerwas, S. and D. Burrell
  1977   "From System to Story." In *Truthfulness and Tragedy*, ed. S. Hauerwas, 15-39. Notre Dame: University of Notre Dame Press.
Haughey, J.
  1981   "Schillebeeckx's Christology." *Theology Today* 38 (2): 201-207.
Heidegger, M.
  1962   *Being and Time.* Trans. J. Macquarrie and E. Robinson. Oxford: Blackwell.

Hellwig, M.
1983 "Changing Soteriology in Ecumenical Context: A Catholic Reflection." *CTSA Proceedings* 38: 14-21.
Hick, J.
1982 *God Has Many Names*. Philadelphia: Westminster Press.
1988 "The Non-Absoluteness of Christianity." In *The Myth of Christian Uniqueness*, ed. J. Hick and P. Knitter. Maryknoll: Orbis Books.
Hilkert, M.
1984 "Towards a Theology of Proclamation: Edward Schillebeeckx's Hermeneutics of Tradition as a Foundation for a Theology of Proclamation." Ph.D. diss., Catholic University of America.
1987 "Hermeneutics of History in the Theology of Edward Schillebeeckx." *The Thomist* 51: 97-145.
1992 "St. Thomas Aquinas and the Appeal of Experience: A Response to Kenneth Schmitz." *CTSA Proceedings* 47: 21-25.
Hilkert, M. and R. Schreiter
1989 *The Praxis of Christian Experience: An Introduction to the Theology of Edward Schillebeeckx*. San Francisco: Harper and Row.
Horkheimer, M.
1989 *Critical Theory: Selected Essays*. New York: Continuum.
Horkheimer, M. and T. Adorno
1989 *Dialectic of Enlightenment*. New York: Continuum.
Hudson, W.D.
1985 "Theology and the Intellectual Endeavour of Mankind." *Religious Studies* 21: 21-37.
Hunsinger, G.
1987 "Beyond Literalism and Expressivism." *Modern Theology* 3 (3): 209-23.
1991 *How to Read Karl Barth: The Shape of His Theology*. Oxford: Oxford University Press.
1992 "Hans Frei as Theologian: The Quest for Generous Orthodoxy." *Modern Theology* 8 (2): 103-28.
1993 "Afterword: Hans Frei as Theologian." In *Theology and Narrative: Selected Essays*, ed. G. Hunsinger and W. Placher, 235-70. Oxford: Oxford University Press.
Jacko, D.
1987 "Salvation in the Context of Contemporary Historical Consciousness: The Later Theology of Edward Schillebeeckx." Unpublished Th.D. diss., Regis College.
Jeanrond, W.
1988 *Text and Interpretation as Categories of Theological Thinking*. Trans. T. Wilson. New York: Crossroad.

Johnson, E.
  1992   *Consider Jesus: Waves of Renewal in Christology.* New York:
         Crossroad.
Jones, G.
  1990   "Critical Study: Learning to Live in Holy Insecurity."
         Modern Theology 6: 385-405.
Josipovici, G.
  1990   "The Bible in Focus." *Journal of the Study of Old Testament* 48:
         101-22.
Kay, J.
  1991   "Myth or Narrative?: Bultmann's 'New Testament and
         Mythology' Turns Fifty." *Theology Today* 48: 326-32.
Keesey, D.
  1980   "The Bible and Christian Theology." *Journal of the American
         Academy of Religion* 48 (3): 385-402.
  1987   *Contexts of Criticism.* Palo Alto: Mayfield Publishing.
Kelber, W.
  1988   "Gospel Narrative and Critical Theory." *Biblical Theology
         Bulletin* 18: 130-36.
Kelsey, D.
  1975   *The Uses of Scripture in Recent Theology.* Philadelphia:
         Fortress Press.
  1987   "Biblical Narrative and Theological Anthropology." In
         Scriptural Authority and Narrative Interpretation, ed. Garrett
         Green, 121-43. Philadelphia: Fortress Press.
  1990   "Church Discourse and Public Realm." In *Theology and
         Dialogue: Essays in Conversation with George Lindbeck*, ed.
         B. Marshall, 7-33. Notre Dame: University of Notre Dame
         Press.
Knitter, P.
  1986   *No Other Name: A Critical Survey of Christian Attitudes Toward
         the World Religions.* Maryknoll: Orbis Books.
Kuikman, J.
  1993   "Christology in the Context of Jewish-Christian Relations:
         The Contribution of Edward Schillebeeckx." Unpublished
         Ph.D. diss., University of Saint Michael's College.
Lacugna, C.
  1991   *God, the Trinity and Christian Life.* San Francisco: Harper
         Collins.
Lander, R.
  1987   "Philosophy and the Catholic Experience." *Cross Currents*
         37: 87-92.

Leonard, E.
1990   "Experience as a Source of Theology." *Studies in Religion* 19 (2): 143-62.
Lindbeck, G.
1984   *The Nature of Doctrine.* Philadelphia: Westminster Press.
1986   "Barth and Textuality." *Theology Today* 43: 361-76.
1988   "The Church." In *Keeping the Faith,* ed. G. Wainwright, 179-208. Philadelphia: Fortress Press.
1989a   "The Church's Mission in a Postmodern Culture." In *Postmodern Theology: Christian Faith in a Pluralist World,* ed. F.B. Burnham, 37-55. San Francisco: Harper and Row.
1989b   "Scripture, Consensus and Community." In *Biblical Interpretation in Crisis,* ed. R. Neuhaus, 74-101. Grand Rapids: Eerdman's Publishing Company.
Lockhead, D.
1988   *The Dialogical Imperative.* Maryknoll: Orbis Books.
Lonergan, B.
1958   *Insight: A Study of Human Understanding.* New York: Longmans, Green and Company.
1972   *Method in Theology.* New York: Herder and Herder.
1985   *A Third Collection: Papers by Bernard J.F. Lonergan, S.J.,* ed. F.E. Crowe. New York: Paulist Press.
Lowe, W.
1992   "Hans Frei and Phenomenological Hermeneutics." *Modern Theology* 8 (2): 133-44.
Macquarrie, J.
1955   *An Existentialist Theology: A Comparison of Heidegger and Bultmann.* London: SCM Press.
1967   *God-Talk.* New York: Harper and Row.
1977   *Principles of Christian Theology.* 2nd ed. New York: Charles Scribner's Sons.
1978   *The Humility of God.* London: SCM Press.
1982   *In Search of Humanity: A Theological and Philosophical Approach.* London: SCM Press.
1984   *In Search of Deity: An Essay in Dialectical Theism.* London: SCM Press.
1990   *Jesus Christ in Modern Thought.* London: SCM Press.
Marcuse, H.
1992   "Philosophy and Critical Theory." In *Critical Theory: The Essential Readings,* ed. D. Ingram and J. Simon-Ingram, 5-19. New York: Paragon House.
Marshall, B.
1987   *Christology in Conflict: The Identity of a Saviour in Rahner and Barth.* Oxford: Basil Blackwell.

1992   "Meaning and Truth in Narrative Interpretation: A Reply to George Schner." *Modern Theology* 8 (2): 173-180.

McCarthy, M.
1992   "The Critique of Realism." *Method: Journal of Lonergan Studies* 10: 89-125.

McKnight, E.V.
1988   *Postmodern Use of the Bible: The Emergence of Reader-Oriented Criticism*. Nashville: Abingdon Press.

Monk, R.
1991   *Ludwig Wittgenstein: The Duty of Genius*. London: Vintage.

Morgan, R. and J. Barton
1988   *Biblical Interpretation*. Oxford: Oxford University Press.

Niebuhr, H.R.
1941   *The Meaning of Revelation*. New York: Macmillan Publishing Company.

Nijenhuis, J.
1980   "Christology Without Jesus of Nazareth Is Ideology: A Monumental Work by Schillebeeckx on Jesus." *Journal of Ecumenical Studies* 17: 125-40.

Nolan, A.
1988   *God in South Africa: The Challenge of the Gospel*. Johannesburg: David Philip.

O'Donovan, L.
1982   "Salvation as the Center of Theology." *Interpretation* 36: 192-96.
1983   "The Ethical Implications of Schillebeeckx's Christology." *CTSA Proceedings* 38: 119-22.

Palmer, R.
1969   *Hermeneutics*. Evanston: Northwestern University Press.

Pauw, A.
1993   "The Word Is Near You: A Feminist Conversation with Lindbeck." *Theology Today* 50 (1): 45-55.

Pieris, A.
1986   *An Asian Theology of Liberation*. Maryknoll: Orbis Books.

Placher, W.
1978   "Scripture as Realistic Narrative: Some Preliminary Questions." *Perspectives in Religious Studies* 5: 32-41.
1987   "Paul Ricoeur and Postliberal Theology: A Conflict of Interpretations." *Modern Theology* 4: 35-52.
1989a   "Hans Frei and the Meaning of Biblical Narrative." *The Christian Century* 106 (18): 556-559.
1989b   "Postliberal Theology." In *The Modern Theologian*, Vol. II, ed. D. Ford, 115-25. Oxford: Basil Blackwell.
1992   "A Modest Response to Paul Schwartzentruber." *Modern Theology* 8 (2): 197-202.

1994 "Gospel's End: Plurality and Ambiguity in Biblical Narratives." *Modern Theology* 10 (2): 143-63.

Poland, L.
1985 "The New Criticism, Neo-Orthodoxy, and the New Testament." *Journal of Religion* 65: 459-77.

Portier, W.
1983 "Schillebeeckx's Dialogue with Critical Theory." *The Ecumenist* XXI (2): 20-27.

1984 "Edward Schillebeeckx as Critical Theorist: The Impact of Neo-Marxist Social Thought on His Recent Theology." *The Thomist* 48: 341-67.

Powell, M.A.
1990 *What Is Narrative Criticism?* Minneapolis: Fortress Press.

Pratt, D.
1988 "God in Action and Interaction." *The Asia Journal of Theology* 2 (1): 459-68.

Race, A.
1983 *Christian and Religious Pluralism.* London: SCM Press.

Ruether, R.R.
1974 *Faith and Fratricide: The Theological Roots of Anti-Semitism.* New York: Seabury Press.

1975 *New Woman, New Earth: Sexist Ideologies and Human Liberation.* New York: Seabury Press.

1983 *Sexism and God-Talk: Toward a Feminist Theology.* Boston: Beacon Press.

1992 *Gaia and God: An Ecofeminist Theology of Earth Healing.* San Francisco: Harper Collins.

Ricoeur, P.
1976 *Interpretation Theory: Discourse and the Surplus of Meaning.* Fort Worth: Texas Christian University Press.

1981 *Hermeneutics and the Human Sciences.* Ed. and trans. J.B. Thompson. Cambridge: Cambridge University Press.

Root, M.
1986 "The Narrative Structure of Soteriology." *Modern Theology* 2 (2): 145-58.

Runyon, T.
1992 "The Role of Experience in Religion." *International Journal for Philosophy of Religion* 31: 187-94.

Russell, L.
1986 *Household of Freedom.* Philadelphia: Westminster Press.

Ryle, G.
1949 *The Concept of Mind.* New York: Penguin Books.

Said, E.
1993 *Culture and Imperialism.* New York: Alfred A. Knopf.

Scheffczyk, L.
1984   "Christology in the Context of Experience: An Interpretation of Christ by Edward Schillebeeckx." *The Thomist* 48: 383-408.

Schillebeeckx, Edward
1963   *Christ, the Sacrament of the Encounter with God.* New York: Sheed and Ward.

1967   *Revelation and Theology I.* New York: Sheed and Ward.

1968a *Revelation and Theology II.* New York: Sheed and Ward.

1968b *The Eucharist.* London: Sheed and Ward.

1971   *World and Church.* London: Sheed and Ward.

1972   "The Christian and Political Engagement." *Doctrine and Life* 22: 118-27.

1973a "Critical Theories and Christian Political Commitment." *Concilium* 84: 48-61.

1973b *The Mission of the Church.* London: Sheed and Ward.

1974   "The 'God of Jesus' and the 'Jesus of God.'" *Concilium* 93: 110-26.

1975a "The Mystery of Injustice and the Mystery of Mercy." *Stauros Bulletin* 3: 3-31.

1975b *The Understanding of Faith.* London: The Catholic Book Club.

1976   "Interdisciplinarity in Theology." *Theology Digest* 24: 137-42.

1977   *God, the Future of Man.* 2nd ed. London: Sheed and Ward.

1978a "God, Society and Human Salvation." In *Faith and Society: Acta Congressus Internationalis Theologici Lovaniensis,* ed. M. Caudron, J. Duculot, 1976: 87-99. Gembloux.

1978b "Questions on Christian Salvation of and for Man." In *Toward Vatican III: The Work that Needs to Be Done,* ed. D. Tracy, H. Küng and J. Metz, 27-44. New York: Seabury Press.

1979   *Jesus: An Experiment in Christology.* New York: Crossroad.

1980a "Can Christology Be an Experiment?" *Proceedings of the Catholic Theological Society of America* 35: 1-14.

1980b *Christ: The Experience of Jesus as Lord.* New York: Crossroad.

1980c "I Believe in Jesus of Nazareth: The Christ, the Son of God, the Lord." *Journal of Ecumenical Studies* 17: 18-32.

1980d "Liberation Theology Between Medellin and Puebla." *Theology Digest* 28: 3-7.

1981a "God, the Living One." *New Blackfriars* 62 (7): 357-69.

1981b *Interim Report on the Books Jesus and Christ.* New York: Crossroad.

1982a "Christian Identity and Human Integrity." *Concilium* 155: 23-31.

1982b "The Magisterium and Ideology." *Journal of Ecumenical Studies* 19: 5-17.

1983   *God Is New Each Moment.* Edinburgh: T. & T. Clark.

1985 *The Church with a Human Face: A New and Expanded Theology of Ministry.* New York: Crossroad.

1987 *Jesus in Our Western Culture: Mysticism, Ethics and Politics.* London: SCM Press.

1989a "The Religious and the Human Ecumene." In *The Future of Liberation Theology: Essays in Honor of Gustavo Gutiérrez,* ed. M. Ellis and O. Maduro, 177-88. Maryknoll: Orbis Books.

1989b "The Role of History in What Is Called the New Paradigm." In *Paradigm Change in Theology,* ed. H. Küng and D. Tracy, trans. M. Köhl, 307-19. New York: Crossroad.

1990 *Church: The Human Story of God.* New York: Crossroad.

1995 *The Language of Faith.* Maryknoll: Orbis Books.

Schmitz, K.

1992 "St. Thomas and the Appeal to Experience." *CTSA Proceedings* 47: 1-20.

Schneiders, S.

1992 "Living Word or Deadly Letter: The Encounter Between the New Testament and Contemporary Experience." *CTSA Proceedings* 47: 45-60.

Schner, G.

1992a "The Appeal to Experience." *Theological Studies* 53: 40-59.

1992b "The Eclipse of Biblical Narrative: Analysis and Critique." *Modern Theology* 8 (2): 149-72.

Schoof, T.

1984 *The Schillebeeckx Case.* Ed. T. Schoof. New York: Paulist Press.

Schreiter, R.

1984 *The Schillebeeckx Reader.* Ed. R. Schreiter. New York: Crossroad.

1986 *Constructing Local Theologies.* Maryknoll: Orbis Books.

Schwartzentruber, P.

1992 "The Modesty of Hermeneutics: The Theological Reserves of Hans Frei." *Modern Theology* 8 (2): 181-96.

Segundo, J.

1988 *Liberation of Theology.* Maryknoll: Orbis Books.

Soelle, D.

1974 *Political Theology.* Trans. J. Shelley. Philadelphia: Fortress Press.

Stroup, G.

1986 "Narrative in Calvin's Hermeneutic." In *Calvin Studies III,* ed. J. Leith, 21-32. Davidson, NC: Davidson Publications.

Swidler, L.

1990 *After the Absolute: The Dialogical Future of Religious Reflection.* Minneapolis: Fortress Press.

Sykes, J.
1989   "Narrative Accounts of Biblical Authority: The Need for a Doctrine of Revelation." *Modern Theology* 5: 327-42.
Tanner, K.
1988   *God and Creation in Christian Theology.* Oxford: Basil Blackwell.
Thatcher, A.
1976   "Concepts of Deity: A Criticism of H.P. Owen." *Anglican Theological Review* 58: 294-306.
Thieman, R.
1986   "Response to Lindbeck." *Theology Today* 43: 377-82.
Thiselton, A.
1980   *The Two Horizons.* Grand Rapids: Eerdmans Publishing Company.
Thomas, O.
1985   "Theology and Experience." Harvard Theological Review 78: 179-201.
Thompson, J.
1978   *Christ in Perspective: Christological Perspectives in the Theology of Karl Barth.* Edinburgh: St. Andrew Press.
Tillich, P.
1951-56 *Systematic Theology.* 3 vols. Chicago: University of Chicago Press.
Tilly, T.
1994   "The Institutional Element in Religious Experience." *Modern Theology* 10 (2): 185-212.
Tolbert, M.
1983   "Defining the Problem: The Bible and Feminist Hermeneutics." *Semeia* 28: 113-26.
Tracy, D.
1975   *Blessed Rage for Order: The New Pluralism in Theology.* New York: Seabury Press.
1987a   *The Analogical Imagination.* New York: Crossroad.
1987b   *Pluralism and Ambiguity: Hermeneutics, Religion and Hope.* San Francisco: Harper and Row.
Trible, P.
1984   *Texts of Terror: Literary-Feminist Readings of Biblical Narratives.* Philadelphia: Fortress Press.
Vidales, R.
1979   "Methodological Issues in Liberation Theology." In *Frontiers of Theology in Latin America*, ed. R. Gibellini, trans. J. Drury, 34-57. Maryknoll: Orbis Books.
Wallace, M.
1987   "The New Yale Theology." *Christian Scholar's Review* 17 (2): 154-70.

Webster, J.
    1984   "Edward Schillebeeckx: God Is Always Absolutely New." *Evangel*, 5-8.
    1986   "Atonement, History and Narrative." *Theologische Zeitschrift*, 115-31.
    1992   "Response to George Hunsinger." *Modern Theology* 8 (2): 129-32.
Werpehowski, W.
    1986   "Ad Hoc Apologetics." *Journal of Religion* 66: 282-301.
Wiseman, J.
    1971   "Schillebeeckx and the Ecclesial Function of Critical Negativity." *The Thomist* 35: 207-46.
Wittgenstein, L.
    1953   *Philosophical Investigations*. Trans. G.E.M. Anscombe. Oxford: Basil Blackwell.
    1961   *Tractatus Logico-Philosophicus*. Trans. D. F. Pears and B.F. McGuinness. London: Routledge.
    1980   *Culture and Value*. Trans. Peter Winch. Chicago: University of Chicago Press.
Wyschogrod, E.
    1990   *Saints and Postmodernism: Revisioning Moral Philosophy*. Chicago: University of Chicago Press.

INDEX

Series Published by Wilfrid Laurier University Press for the Canadian Corporation for Studies in Religion / Corporation Canadienne des Sciences Religieuses

Editions SR

1. *La langue de Ya'udi : description et classement de l'ancien parler de Zencircli dans le cadre des langues sémitiques du nord-ouest*
   Paul-Eugène Dion, O.P. / 1974 / viii + 511 p. / OUT OF PRINT
2. *The Conception of Punishment in Early Indian Literature*
   Terence P. Day / 1982 / iv + 328 pp.
3. *Traditions in Contact and Change: Selected Proceedings of the XIVth Congress of the International Association for the History of Religions*
   Edited by Peter Slater and Donald Wiebe with Maurice Boutin and Harold Coward
   1983 / x + 758 pp. / OUT OF PRINT
4. *Le messianisme de Louis Riel*
   Gilles Martel / 1984 / xviii + 483 p.
5. *Mythologies and Philosophies of Salvation in the Theistic Traditions of India*
   Klaus K. Klostermaier / 1984 / xvi + 549 pp. / OUT OF PRINT
6. *Averroes' Doctrine of Immortality: A Matter of Controversy*
   Ovey N. Mohammed / 1984 / vi + 202 pp. / OUT OF PRINT
7. *L'étude des religions dans les écoles : l'expérience américaine, anglaise et canadienne*
   Fernand Ouellet / 1985 / xvi + 666 p.
8. *Of God and Maxim Guns: Presbyterianism in Nigeria, 1846-1966*
   Geoffrey Johnston / 1988 / iv + 322 pp.
9. *A Victorian Missionary and Canadian Indian Policy: Cultural Synthesis vs Cultural Replacement*
   David A. Nock / 1988 / x + 194 pp. / OUT OF PRINT
10. *Prometheus Rebound: The Irony of Atheism*
    Joseph C. McLelland / 1988 / xvi + 366 pp.
11. *Competition in Religious Life*
    Jay Newman / 1989 / viii + 237 pp.
12. *The Huguenots and French Opinion, 1685-1787: The Enlightenment Debate on Toleration*
    Geoffrey Adams / 1991 / xiv + 335 pp.
13. *Religion in History: The Word, the Idea, the Reality / La religion dans l'histoire : le mot, l'idée, la réalité*
    Edited by/Sous la direction de Michel Despland and /et Gérard Vallée
    1992 / x + 252 pp.
14. *Sharing Without Reckoning: Imperfect Right and the Norms of Reciprocity*
    Millard Schumaker / 1992 / xiv + 112 pp.
15. *Love and the Soul: Psychological Interpretations of the Eros and Psyche Myth*
    James Gollnick / 1992 / viii + 174 pp.
16. *The Promise of Critical Theology: Essays in Honour of Charles Davis*
    Edited by Marc P. Lalonde / 1995 / xii + 146 pp.
17. *The Five Aggregates: Understanding Theravāda Psychology and Soteriology*
    Mathieu Boisvert / 1995 / xii + 166 pp.

18. *Mysticism and Vocation*
    James R. Horne / 1996 / vi + 110 pp.
19. *Memory and Hope: Strands of Canadian Baptist History*
    Edited by David T. Priestley / 1996 / viii + 211 pp.
20. *The Concept of Equity in Calvin's Ethics**
    Guenther H. Haas / 1997 / xii + 205 pp.
    * Available in the United Kingdom and Europe from Paternoster Press.
21. *The Call of Conscience: French Protestant Responses to the Algerian War, 1954-1962*
    Geoffrey Adams / 1998 / xxii + 270 pp.
22. *Clinical Pastoral Supervision and the Theology of Charles Gerkin*
    Thomas St. James O'Connor / 1998 / x + 152 pp.
23. *Faith and Fiction: A Theological Critique of the Narrative Strategies of Hugh MacLennan and Morley Callaghan*
    Barbara Pell / 1998 / v + 141 pp.
24. *God and the Chip: Religion and the Culture of Technology*
    William A. Stahl / 1999 / vi + 186 pp.
25. *The Religious Dreamworld of Apuleius' Metamorphoses: Recovering a Forgotten Hermeneutic*
    James Gollnick / 1999 / xiv + 178 pp.
26. *Edward Schillebeeckx and Hans Frei: A Conversation on Method and Christology*
    Marguerite Abdul-Masih / 2001 / vi + 194 pp.
27. *Radical Difference: A Defence of Hendrik Kraemer's Theology of Religions*
    Tim S. Perry / 2001 / x + 170 pp.

Comparative Ethics Series / Collection d'Éthique Comparée

1. *Muslim Ethics and Modernity: A Comparative Study of the Ethical Thought of Sayyid Ahmad Khan and Mawlana Mawdudi*
   Sheila McDonough / 1984 / x + 130 pp. / OUT OF PRINT
2. *Methodist Education in Peru: Social Gospel, Politics, and American Ideological and Economic Penetration, 1888-1930*
   Rosa del Carmen Bruno-Jofré / 1988 / xiv + 223 pp.
3. *Prophets, Pastors and Public Choices: Canadian Churches and the Mackenzie Valley Pipeline Debate*
   Roger Hutchinson / 1992 / xiv + 142 pp. / OUT OF PRINT
4. *In Good Faith: Canadian Churches Against Apartheid*
   Renate Pratt / 1997 / xii + 366 pp.
5. *Towards an Ethics of Community: Negotiations of Difference in a Pluralist Society*
   James H. Olthuis, editor / 2000 / x + 230 pp.

Dissertations SR

1. *The Social Setting of the Ministry as Reflected in the Writings of Hermas, Clement and Ignatius*
   Harry O. Maier / 1991 / viii + 230 pp. / OUT OF PRINT
2. *Literature as Pulpit: The Christian Social Activism of Nellie L. McClung*
   Randi R. Warne / 1993 / viii + 236 pp. / OUT OF PRINT

Studies in Christianity and Judaism / Études sur le christianisme et le judaïsme

1. *A Study in Anti-Gnostic Polemics: Irenaeus, Hippolytus, and Epiphanius*
   Gérard Vallée / 1981 / xii + 114 pp. / OUT OF PRINT
2. *Anti-Judaism in Early Christianity*
   Vol. 1, *Paul and the Gospels*
   Edited by Peter Richardson with David Granskou / 1986 / x + 232 pp.

Vol. 2, *Separation and Polemic*
Edited by Stephen G. Wilson / 1986 / xii + 185 pp.
3. *Society, the Sacred, and Scripture in Ancient Judaism: A Sociology of Knowledge*
Jack N. Lightstone / 1988 / xiv + 126 pp.
4. *Law in Religious Communities in the Roman Period: The Debate Over* **Torah** *and* **Nomos**
in Post-Biblical Judaism and Early Christianity
Peter Richardson and Stephen Westerholm with A. I. Baumgarten, Michael Pettem
and Cecilia Wassén / 1991 / x + 164 pp.
5. *Dangerous Food: 1 Corinthians 8-10 in Its Context*
Peter D. Gooch / 1993 / xviii + 178 pp.
6. *The Rhetoric of the Babylonian Talmud, Its Social Meaning and Context*
Jack N. Lightstone / 1994 / xiv + 317 pp.
7. *Whose Historical Jesus?*
Edited by William E. Arnal and Michel Desjardins / 1997 / vi + 337 pp.
8. *Religious Rivalries and the Struggle for Success in Caesarea Maritima*
Edited by Terence L. Donaldson / 2000 / xiv + 402 pp.
9. *Text and Artifact in the Religions of Mediterranean Antiquity*
Edited by Stephen G. Wilson and Michel Desjardins / 2000 / xvi + 616 pp.
10. *Parables of War: Reading John's Jewish Apocalypse*
by John W. Marshall / 2001 / 256 pp. est.

The Study of Religion in Canada /
Sciences Religieuses au Canada

1. *Religious Studies in Alberta: A State-of-the-Art Review*
Ronald W. Neufeldt / 1983 / xiv + 145 pp.
2. *Les sciences religieuses au Québec depuis 1972*
Louis Rousseau et Michel Despland / 1988 / 158 p.
3. *Religious Studies in Ontario: A State-of-the-Art Review*
Harold Remus, William Closson James and Daniel Fraikin / 1992 / xviii + 422 pp.
4. *Religious Studies in Manitoba and Saskatchewan: A State-of-the-Art Review*
John M. Badertscher, Gordon Harland and Roland E. Miller / 1993 / vi + 166 pp.
5. *The Study of Religion in British Columbia: A State-of-the-Art Review*
Brian J. Fraser / 1995 / x + 127 pp.
6. *Religious Studies in Atlantic Canada: A State-of-the-Art Review*
Paul W.R. Bowlby with Tom Faulkner / 2001 / xii + 208 pp.

Studies in Women and Religion /
Études sur les femmes et la religion

1. *Femmes et religions**
Sous la direction de Denise Veillette / 1995 / xviii + 466 p.
* Only available from Les Presses de l'Université Laval
2. *The Work of Their Hands: Mennonite Women's Societies in Canada*
Gloria Neufeld Redekop / 1996 / xvi + 172 pp.
3. *Profiles of Anabaptist Women: Sixteenth-Century Reforming Pioneers*
Edited by C. Arnold Snyder and Linda A. Huebert Hecht / 1996 / xxii + 438 pp.
4. *Voices and Echoes: Canadian Women's Spirituality*
Edited by Jo-Anne Elder and Colin O'Connell / 1997 / xxviii + 237 pp.
5. *Obedience, Suspicion and the Gospel of Mark: A Mennonite-Feminist Exploration of Biblical
Authority*
Lydia Neufeld Harder / 1998 / xiv + 168 pp.
6. *Clothed in Integrity: Weaving Just Cultural Relations and the Garment Industry*
Barbara Paleczny / 2000 / xxxiv + 352 pp.

SR Supplements

1. *Footnotes to a Theology: The Karl Barth Colloquium of 1972*
   Edited and Introduced by Martin Rumscheidt / 1974 / viii + 151 pp. / OUT OF PRINT
2. *Martin Heidegger's Philosophy of Religion*
   John R. Williams / 1977 / x + 190 pp. / OUT OF PRINT
3. *Mystics and Scholars: The Calgary Conference on Mysticism 1976*
   Edited by Harold Coward and Terence Penelhum / 1977 / viii + 121 pp. / OUT OF PRINT
4. *God's Intention for Man: Essays in Christian Anthropology*
   William O. Fennell / 1977 / xii + 56 pp. / OUT OF PRINT
5. *"Language" in Indian Philosophy and Religion*
   Edited and Introduced by Harold G. Coward / 1978 / x + 98 pp. / OUT OF PRINT
6. *Beyond Mysticism*
   James R. Horne / 1978 / vi + 158 pp. / OUT OF PRINT
7. *The Religious Dimension of Socrates' Thought*
   James Beckman / 1979 / xii + 276 pp. / OUT OF PRINT
8. *Native Religious Traditions*
   Edited by Earle H. Waugh and K. Dad Prithipaul / 1979 / xii + 244 pp. / OUT OF PRINT
9. *Developments in Buddhist Thought: Canadian Contributions to Buddhist Studies*
   Edited by Roy C. Amore / 1979 / iv + 196 pp.
10. *The Bodhisattva Doctrine in Buddhism*
    Edited and Introduced by Leslie S. Kawamura / 1981 / xxii + 274 pp. / OUT OF PRINT
11. *Political Theology in the Canadian Context*
    Edited by Benjamin G. Smillie / 1982 / xii + 260 pp.
12. *Truth and Compassion: Essays on Judaism and Religion in Memory of Rabbi Dr. Solomon Frank*
    Edited by Howard Joseph, Jack N. Lightstone and Michael D. Oppenheim
    1983 / vi + 217 pp. / OUT OF PRINT
13. *Craving and Salvation: A Study in Buddhist Soteriology*
    Bruce Matthews / 1983 / xiv + 138 pp. / OUT OF PRINT
14. *The Moral Mystic*
    James R. Horne / 1983 / x + 134 pp.
15. *Ignatian Spirituality in a Secular Age*
    Edited by George P. Schner / 1984 / viii + 128 pp. / OUT OF PRINT
16. *Studies in the Book of Job*
    Edited by Walter E. Aufrecht / 1985 / xii + 76 pp.
17. *Christ and Modernity: Christian Self-Understanding in a Technological Age*
    David J. Hawkin / 1985 / x + 181 pp.
18. *Young Man Shinran: A Reappraisal of Shinran's Life*
    Takamichi Takahatake / 1987 / xvi + 228 pp. / OUT OF PRINT
19. *Modernity and Religion*
    Edited by William Nicholls / 1987 / vi + 191 pp.
20. *The Social Uplifters: Presbyterian Progressives and the Social Gospel in Canada, 1875-1915*
    Brian J. Fraser / 1988 / xvi + 212 pp. / OUT OF PRINT

Series discontinued

Available from:

Wilfrid Laurier University Press

Waterloo, Ontario, Canada   N2L 3C5
Telephone: (519) 884-0710, ext. 6124
Fax: (519) 725-1399
E-mail: press@wlu.ca
World Wide Web: http://www.wlu.ca/~wwwpress/